BRIGHT NOTES

THE FELLOWSHIP OF THE RING BY J.R.R. TOLKIEN

Intelligent Education

Nashville, Tennessee

BRIGHT NOTES: The Fellowship of the Ring
www.BrightNotes.com

No part of this publication may be used or reproduced in any manner whatsoever without written permission, except in the case of brief quotations in critical articles and reviews. For permissions, contact Influence Publishers http://www.influencepublishers.com.

ISBN: 978-1-645422-96-9 (Paperback)
ISBN: 978-1-645422-97-6 (eBook)

Published in accordance with the U.S. Copyright Office Orphan Works and Mass Digitization report of the register of copyrights, June 2015.

Originally published by Monarch Press.
Louise D. Morrison, 1976
2019 Edition published by Influence Publishers.

Interior design by Lapiz Digital Services. Cover Design by Thinkpen Designs.

Printed in the United States of America.

Library of Congress Cataloging-in-Publication Data forthcoming.
Names: Intelligent Education
Title: BRIGHT NOTES: The Fellowship of the Ring
Subject: STU004000 STUDY AIDS / Book Notes

CONTENTS

1)	Introduction to J. R. R. Tolkien	1
2)	Textual Analysis	
	Themes and Techniques in "The Fellowship of The Ring"	22
	Part 1	40
	Part 2	62
	Part 3	80
3)	Characterization and Critics	95
4)	Essay Questions and Answers	116
5)	Topics for Research and Criticism	124
6)	Bibliography	127

INTRODUCTION TO J. R. R. TOLKIEN

J. R. R. Tolkien's massive literary labor of producing *The Lord of the Rings* evidences his dogged persistence in creating a twentieth-century masterpiece despite his demanding responsibilities as a tutor at Oxford. Elves, dwarves, hobbits, and other supernatural creatures move through a chronicle which is unique in modern literature. The trilogy owes an enormous debt to the Nordic sagas, lays and eddas, containing a wealth of the ancient lore of Northern Europeans. *The Lord of the Rings* is quintessentially a Nordic myth.

The story takes place in the Third Age of Middle Earth, a Tolkien term for a fantasy period of time in ancient days when men mingled with other creatures of different species and even intermarried. Tolkien has created an area with its own particular geography, a history all its own, detailed genealogies, ballads, elaborately drawn maps, and intriguing myths. In addition, he has invented several different languages, obviously the legacies of ancient Welsh and Anglo-Saxon. Even extraordinary fantastic flowers and trees dot the landscape of Tolkien's world.

While nowhere in the work does the author intrude subjectively - in fact, he insists he is merely reporting from the chronicle in the *Red Book of Westmarch* - the world that Tolkien creates is Tolkien himself. A profound scholar of Scandinavian and Middle English with a special bent toward linguistics, philology, and etymology, the author has come up with his own myth couched appropriately in tongues of his own creation. Readers everywhere, especially young people, immerse themselves gladly in the fascinating Third Age of Middle Earth where heroes once again stride across the horizon, filling a present-day cultural gap. Tolkien has achieved tremendous popularity as a spinner of tall tales about heroic ventures. But there is more to this author than that. He uses his trilogy as a vehicle to convey his beliefs about Life and Death and Good and Evil. Tolkien's creations and his own world are inseparable, the art being so closely interwoven with his own career and life work. Both the man and the work are indeed distinctive in the contemporary world.

TOLKIEN'S EARLY LIFE

Family Background and Influence

John Ronald Reuel Tolkien distinguished himself from most of his fellow Englishmen by being born in Bloemfontain, South Africa, in 1892. Located in the open, grassy country in high veld, the capital city of the Orange Free State, with its clearaired, invigorating climate, spreads over the hills in a naturally beautiful setting which justifies the meaning of its name, "fountain of flowers." Tolkien's love for idyllic, pastoral scenes must surely have generated from his birthplace.

His mother had held the unusual position of missionary to the women of the Sultan of Zanzibar, an island which lies only a shallow channel away from Africa's East Coast. She had many extraordinary adventures to relate from her missionary work. Her maiden name was Mabel Suffield. Tolkien's father, the son of a well-entrenched British family, was pursuing his career as a bank merchant when his first child was born. Though the child Tolkien was physically weak, he was strong in his Saxon heritage which he later loved and learned in depth. Bloemfontain, in the last decade of the nineteenth century before the battles, concentration camps, and other atrocities of the present century, paralleled the peaceful colony which the hobbits contentedly inhabited before the threat of doom overshadowed their rural haven.

Tolkien himself recalled little of his own life in Bloemfontain. Only two incidents clung to his mind. On one occasion a black native kidnapped the very small boy to show him off to his fellow tribesman in his kraal as a white child. Despite the fright of his parents, no scars from the unnerving episode marked the boy. The other event Tolkien was able to recall featured a snake which appeared in the garden of the Tolkien home, somehow conjuring up images of the first serpent in the Garden of Eden. The child managed to escape a snake bite but he was stung by a tarantula as he was running through the tall, dried grass on a sizzling, sunny day.

Ill health concluded Tolkien's early years in Africa. His mother took him to England when he was four, leaving the senior Tolkien behind. The son never saw his father again because the bank merchant died prematurely a year later in 1896. This loss indelibly marked the frail boy's childhood. The shadow of sorrow no doubt increased his natural reserve and pensiveness though he did not resort to creating his own world until he was an adult.

Even as a child Tolkien found languages fascinating and set out on his way to develop several of his own. His pleasure-filled if unusual occupation with inventing languages came to an abrupt halt as his mother grew concerned over her son's extraordinary interest.

Tolkien's England

In England the Tolkiens lived in a village, Sarehole, near Birmingham in Warwickshire, a middle county as far as possible from the sea. This haven-like home, so far inland, was sheltered from the dangers of the waters which have always plagued England. However, highly developed industry in the Birmingham area threatened the pastoral beauty of nearby Avon which Shakespeare had loved and praised in his works.

Tolkien's transplantation to another world brought sharp contrasts - the heat of Africa as opposed to the damp fog of Warwickshire. As an old man the author recalled his childhood as full of tragedies - his father's death, his own frailty, and his move from his birthplace to an alien country where he paradoxically belonged. A brother who later became an apple farmer provided companionship for Tolkien though principally he led the life of a loner. His mother's tales at lonely times fostered his love for romance and philology. His mother had become a teacher, enabling the family to live not unpleasantly in genteel poverty in the days before World War I rained the initial attacks of doom on the British Empire.

Catholicism

The family conversion to the Catholic Church occurred when Tolkien was quite young, probably around the time of his father's death. Orthodox religion had a strongly discernible impact on him as a boy. Perhaps the sorrows he encountered before reaching adulthood inclined him to depend on his religious faith. The death of his mother in 1910 brought yet another grief to the eighteen-year-old Tolkien. He remained close to his church all his life.

Education

Tolkien shortly followed the British educational tradition. He entered King Edward's Grammar School as a competent day student able to make his way on scholarship. His guardian, Francis Xavier Morgan, was serving as a priest at the Birmingham Oratory. The half-Spanish surrogate father enriched Tolkien's spiritual life, instilling into the young man a practice of Catholicism which would never leave him. John Henry, Cardinal Newman, had founded the Birmingham Oratory. In Tolkien's time as a student there, the school was lagging into deep decline, pervaded by an atmosphere of rejection of Catholics.

Nevertheless, King Edward's School paved the way for a scholarship at Oxford. Tolkien entered Exeter College, Oxford, as an exhibitioner in 1911 and passed Classical Moderations in 1913, having laid the foundations for his later scholarly absorptions. Tolkien was graduated at the age of twenty-three in 1915. The adult world he moved into was at war. In this respect Tolkien, no different from others of his generation, answered the call to the colors.

A love affair and subsequent marriage softened the brunt of war. The object of Tolkien's affections was Edith Bratt. Her guardians frowned on Tolkien as a prospective husband, objecting to his Catholicism and his unstable future. But, like many wartime lovers, the young couple married despite objections. Their long life together attested to their devotion.

WAR YEARS AND AFTERMATH

Military Service

Tolkien, the young bridegroom and recent graduate, assumed a sacrificial role in World War I as an infantry soldier in the Lancasshire Fusiliers where mortality rates soared. His well-known remark at the war's end indicated that he had only one friend left when hostilities concluded, a sorrowful burden to the heart of one who treasured friendships but found them elusive.

Tolkien himself was wounded in the trenches of the Western front around Bapaume in the Franco-English deadlock with the Germans. A protracted stay in a British hospital bed, regaining his health, brought forth the burgeoning of Tolkien's life-long commitment to language. Lying in thought for long days and nights of recovery, Tolkien resolved to learn language with all its ramifications of the roots of words and their derivations. His convalescence undoubtedly distilled his war experiences into firm memories which have emerged later in his trilogy - for example, the deep comradeships which flourished in acutely dangerous circumstances. It is likely that at this time Tolkien's mind began to spin out The Silmarillion and the "Ball of Gondolin." While World War I proved an uncomfortable ordeal, it also served as the experience from which Tolkien chose what he would become and what kind of a life he would lead.

Graduate Work

At school Tolkien had already developed a keen liking for history, botany, grammar, and the study of words with a special eye to linguistics, that brand of language study which recognizes inherent meaning in sounds. It is not surprising that in 1919 Tolkien received another scholarship and was awarded Master of Arts and the Diploma of Comparative Philology. Then, for two years, he served as an assistant on the Oxford English Dictionary, that set of tomes delving into the essence of the English language itself. In revising the dictionary, Tolkien worked closely with words, tracing the beginnings, the original uses, and the transitions incurred in time.

Professorial Years

In 1921, with a young family already started, Tolkien began the years of teaching at which he became a recognized master. His academic career started at the University of Leeds in 1921 where he was Reader in the English Language. In 1922 he published A Middle English Vocabulary. He became Professor of English Language in a short four years as he entered his thirties. The position in England carries great prestige since each department generally has only one professor, the chairman. A call from Oxford promptly followed on the heels of the professorship.

In 1925 Tolkien became Rawlinson and Bosworth Professor of Anglo-Saxon at Pembroke College, Oxford, and that same year an outstanding version of *Sir Gawain and the Green Knight* which he had edited with E. V. Gordon appeared. In 1926 he won a fellowship at Pembroke College, a post he was to hold until 1945. So, from 1925 to 1945 he thrived amid the tradition-laden halls of Oxford, functioning effectively in the male society of the college system with constant tutorial duties, companionship with the students in dining together, joking, gossiping and, in general, enjoying a unique type of comradeship.

Progress in Academia

"Chaucer as a Philologist," which Tolkien presented in 1934 to the Philological Society, marked an academic milestone. He studied as a Leverthulme Research Fellow for two years from 1934 to 1936. In 1936 he matriculated at Exeter College from which he earned a Master of Arts to be awarded in 1944. 1936 was a high-water mark in Tolkien's professorial years. He delivered an address, "Beowulf: The Monsters and the Critics," which brought new life to the ancient Anglo-Saxon **epic**, girding the saga of heroes and dragons with a refreshing appreciation of the re-creation of another world as real as the everyday world of only men. Tolkien had already learned the force of mythology as a tool for viewing reality.

His approach to the monsters in *Beowulf*, Grendel and Grendel's mother, forecast Tolkien's own use of monsters as the personification of evil. These dragons, mythic enlargements of the biblical serpent in Eden, represent the enemy of God and man alike. In the age-old struggle man can never hope to win but he can emerge as a hero endowed with courage and free will. Tolkien immediately established himself as an eminent scholar.

Role of Professor

Great popularity flowed into the Professor's life. He enchanted his students by reading Beowulf aloud, the light from the window shining on his fair hair and his dark, flowing academic gown. Though the students did not know the language of the ancient Anglo-Saxons, Tolkien's ability to transmit the bloody encounters, the hazards and perils of their forebears made their spines tingle as they sat fascinated, crowded in lecture rooms. Wispy-haired, a little taller than average, the Professor became a familiar figure, his coat and cardigan slightly rumpled. He frequently bicycled about campus.

Professorial duties claimed an enormous chunk of time. Life as a tutor in Oxford's college system followed a daily routine of getting up about seven, having tea, attending the college chapel, breakfasting, and then answering notes and letters. From nine to ten the professor wrote. Most Oxford dons wrote in longhand and very little revision was necessary to make the first draft ready for printing.

Four hours of tutoring followed before lunch. Students produced weekly essays of about 3,000 words - sometimes more - to be read in tutorial sessions preceding the instruction bouts over omissions and/or corrections. Afternoons remained free for the tutors until five o'clock when additional tutoring took place. Likely as not students would show up for several more hours after dinner. Indeed a busy routine! Yet Tolkien, with his tight schedule and a family to rear, frequently graded papers for other universities. One day a week free brought respite from the extremely structured routine. Despite the demands of his professorial life, Tolkien, the working teacher, managed to maintain an extraordinary degree of creativity, as his published works indicate.

As a professor Tolkien was not without flaws. Ruffling through notes and speaking in a rapid monotone characterized some of his lectures. But once a point of interest occurred to him in a lecture, he became invigorated, brightening and expanding and explaining in infinite detail. His manner in the classroom was light and graceful, endlessly courteous and kind. He was a gentle and truly great teacher who unstintingly gave himself to his work with his students, laboring with each one endeavoring to publish with such absorption that the student's work became his own. This was his pleasure for which he never sought credit.

Literary Fellowship

A highlight of Tolkien's professorial years was his fellowship with the Inklings, a circle of men who met fairly regularly on Thursday or Friday evenings in pubs like the Lamb and Flag or The Eagle and Child or in the rooms of C. S. Lewis, the well-known novelists whom Tolkien aided in his search for God.

In Lewis' rooms at Magdalen College - or wherever - the gathering of six or eight intellectuals, including W. H. Lewis, a brother of Clive (C. S.), Charles Williams, Hugo Dyson, Nevill Coghill, and Gervase Mathew, would enjoy tea. Then, after having lit their pipes, they would relax and read manuscripts. The question, "Well, has anybody got anything to read us?" sparked the dons to pull manuscripts out of their pockets. In this fashion Tolkien's "new Hobbit," as the group called *The Fellowship of the Ring*, found its first audience. The chapters brought criticism of a sturdy, candid type to which the author himself was utterly impervious. C. S. Lewis once remarked, "No one ever influenced Tolkien - you might as well try to influence a baldersnatch." This literary circle of Christians (Anglicans and, in Tolkien's case, a Catholic) has sometimes been called the Oxford Christians but, by whatever name, Tolkien, Williams, and Lewis found success in writing, setting out on literary journeys to create fantasy and romance conveying substantial themes.

Besides the fellowship of the Inklings, Tolkien enjoyed the stimulating company of Helen MacMillan Brockhurst, an Oxford colleague and a godmother in the Tolkien household. She was a distinguished Icelandic scholar, steeped in the ancient sagas, and Norse mythology was her forte.

Honors Abounding

Scholarly achievement crowned Tolkien's work. Honorary degrees flowed his way from University College, Dublin, and from the University of Liege. In 1933 he delivered the W. F. Ker lecture to scholars and students at Glasgow University. "On Fairy Stories" was the title of the Andrew Lang lecture given the Tolkien at St. Andrew's University in 1938. He reaffirmed his concept clearly in this now-published essay: fairy stories are not written for children. He here enhanced his thesis formulated in the Beowulf lecture. He views the story-teller as a sub-creator. Fantasy functions in making other worlds which offer readers three salutary states which Tolkien calls, Recovery, Escape, and Consolation. Recovery recasts one's ability to see the world sharply and clearly in all its wonder. Escape relates to an appreciation of the natural world which modern man tends to lose sight of in technological times. Consolation, which he calls eucatastrophe, provides the happy ending which he likens to the state of joy and grace found in religion. In this lecture Tolkien presented his theory of fantasy which comes to life in his works.

MIDDLE EARTH YEARS

Tolkien as Realist

In spite of all the orcs and trolls and other superhuman creatures who people Tolkien's writing, the man himself was a firm realist. His views of children reflected this. He tossed out the Peter Pan approach, insisting that children grow up. The hazard of losing innocence and a sense of wonder receives amplification from adults themselves in their bungling efforts to hide realities from the very young, Tolkien believed. He asserted that children suffer from being underrated by parents and other adults who deny them the truth. They sentimentalize and sugar-coat materials in stories which pass poorly as children's literature. Tolkien respected the innate innocence of the child. He liked to quote G. K. Chesterton who said: "For children are innocent and love justice while most of us are wicked, and naturally prefer mercy." Bowdlerizing the old stories, diluting their substance into weakened versions offended Tolkien greatly. He believed that children's stories should come off clearly and truthfully with no withholding. If a violent conflict occurred, include it in a story for children. The thought of a good fight put a sparkle in Tolkien's kindly blue eyes. He also believed that if a fairy story was worth its salt, it must be written for and read by adults. With that in mind, fairy-story writers might turn out suitable literature even if, at times, products might be beyond the children's ability to grasp the entity. Such literature would provide healthy growing pains.

Tolkien and Fairy Stories

It was not as a child that Tolkien learned to love fairy stories. He discovered fairy stories at school when sorrow dogged his steps. Then, in his late teens, philology led him to explore old literary works, delving into their authentic meanings. This pursuit developed in him a real fondness for fairy stories. The war years heightened his interest in the genre.

Tolkien, with his natural reserve, never elaborated on why his experience in World War I contributed to his liking of fairy stories. Conjecturing can lead one to suspect that the gross horrors of war and the inhumanity of man to man bred within his spirit a deep longing for an Other World where good and evil stood out as clear cut factors, where justice would prevail. Elements of the fairy story prevail in his works.

"The Hobbit"

Tolkien wrote *The Hobbit* his story about the pint-sized, loving creatures, in the thirties on bits and pieces of paper from notebooks and scraps from legal-sized pads. Tolkien later denied writing the book for his children, claiming that early statement as a cover-up for his own youthful shyness. In writing *The Hobbit* he served his apprenticeship, preparing himself for his major task, *The Lord of The Rings*. The story goes that once, while grading papers, Tolkien happened to write on the back of a blank page, "In a hole in the ground there lived a hobbit." So it all began.

The first audience for this steady best seller-the Tolkien children-numbered four. John became a priest serving the parish of Stoke-on-Trent, a city church. Earlier he served a long stint as chaplain at Keele University in Staffordshire and at the same time ran the local parish. Teaching careers beckoned three of the Tolkien children. Christopher followed his father Oxford where he holds his father's position. He served as a war pilot in the R.A.F., having spent eighteen months in South Africa in 1944–1945. He joined the Naval Air Arm when, after V. E. Day, becoming a Physical Training Equipment Officer seemed an imminent disaster. During Christopher's tour of duty in South Africa, his father mailed him parts of *The Lord of The Rings*. Another son, Michael, teaches for the Jesuits at Stonyhurst in

Lancashire. The one Tolkien daughter, Priscilla, lectures at a technical college.

After having tried *The Hobbit* out on his children, Tolkien read it to his group at Oxford and discovered pleasantly that others considered the material publishable. The publication of the manuscript somehow evolved, to the surprise of its author. An edition with Tolkien's own illustrations appeared in 1938 but the blitz of World War II destroyed this. Other editions have since appeared with various types of illustrations. Translations into many foreign languages followed. Tolkien's illustrations have gradually come into their own and are accepted as the best of the artistic interpretations of *The Hobbit*.

The Hobbit possesses a charm all its own. The book introduced the public to Tolkien's ingenious invention - the hobbit - the diminishing breed of the little folks about two to four feet high with hairy, leathery feet which require not shoes. Distinctly provincial, this party-and-food-loving clan like to live undisturbed in their verdant Shire, smoking their pipe weed and relaxing in comfortable security.

The Hobbit, however, deals with evil. Bilbo Baggins, a fifty-year-old hobbit, joins Thorin Oakinshield and twelve dwarves in their quest to expel Smaug, the dragon, from the Lonely Mountain and to gain back Thorin's treasure and his title as king. Magician Gandalf has chosen Bilbo as the "burglar" for the group. The clearly symbolic forces of good and evil conflict. Elrond, the Elven lord of great power and wisdom, the warrior and bear Beorn and Gandalf emerge as virtuous champions of good. (Beorn's name derives from Anglo-Saxon word for prince.) Trolls, goblins and wargs (this means wolf in Anglo-Saxon) surface as evil figures bent on destruction.

Tolkien neatly balances development and disintegration. Bilbo grows in heroic stature while the age-old sins of avarice and cowardice grip the dwarves, causing moral flabbiness.

A dramatic event lays the groundwork for *The Lord of The Rings*. Bilbo encounters Gollum, a distorted creature representing good turned evil, and obtains the One Ring, symbolic of awesome power. Bilbo faces yet another trial in which temptation wins. He steals the Arkenstone, a jewel of great value, from Smaug who in turn takes to the warpath which culminates in The Battle of the Five Armies.

The Hobbit deals significantly with growing up. Its language reveals the **theme** beginning with Bilbo's hobbit hole which is named Bag End, symbol of the womb. Bilbo finds himself expelled and naked (without a handkerchief) pilgrimaging toward a dragon. Tolkien follows the Jungian interpretation of rebirth as the making of a hero, initiating Bilbo into manhood by literally a trial by fire and symbolic descents into the underworld of dark, secret caves. Bilbo's renouncing the stolen Arkenstone signifies his resurrection, laying the thematic groundwork for *The Lord of the Rings*.

CONTINUING SUCCESS

Tolkien in America

While Tolkien was distinguishing himself as a scholar in his own country, American honorary degrees awaited the professor-author from Marquette, Harvard, and several other universities. His plans to come to America in 1957 to receive the degrees and to deliver a series of lectures failed to materialize due to the illness of his wife. Regrettably Tolkien never came to this country despite extraordinary popularity in the United States. His fame in America overwhelmed and puzzled the retiring English don. His fan mail invited great problems. Tolkien had no secretary to handle such matters and was no hand at delegating tasks at all.

The withdrawn writer experienced genuine astonishment when Richard Plotz, then a senior at Erasmus High School in Brooklyn, later a Harvard student, organized the first Tolkien Society in America. In city after city other groups banded together for a fare of mushrooms, hobbits' favorite food. At least a dozen journals address themselves to Tolkienese matters in interpreting and studying the languages he has invented.

Other Creative Works

Tolkien produced a little story, "Leaf by Niggle," which was ultimately published in a Catholic paper, *The Dublin Review*, in 1947. The world of fantasy beckoned once again and Tolkien carried his little Britisher Niggle, often compared to the author himself, into the world of After Life.

Bogged down with the beginning of the trilogy, Tolkien saw from his bedroom window a popular tree senselessly destroyed. The tree was to become a major symbol for Tolkien, representing abundance and fulfillment. Niggle began his work on canvas with a leaf which grew into a tree. The artist could not complete his work, even as Tolkien, occupied with his busy routine as a tutor, could not finish the trilogy.

Niggle's association with his neighbor Parish brings out the interdependency in human relationships and presents the little work's principal **theme** - the artist's obligation to the community. The growth of Niggle's leaf into a tree with twigs and branches and a forest background sharply parallels Tolkien's work in the expansion of *The Hobbit* into *The Lord of the Rings*.

An underlying factor, the search for holiness, takes Niggle through the stages of purgatory - a testing period, a sojourn in a lovely landscape like that in his own painting, and a final ascent to the unknowable heaven of the Delectable Mountains. Enlargement of this **theme** emerges in the trilogy.

When Tolkien published *Father Giles of Ham* in 1949, he turned his sights to the Middle Ages and the world of myth in the kingdom of an arrogant ruler populated by his petty knights and a real life dragon. Here the Tolkien pattern recurs in the confrontation of persons and monsters. Farmer Giles' dog reincarnates Garm, the remarkable dog of ancient mythology. This amusing short story evidences Tolkien's delightful sense of humor and his ability to ridicule his own linguistic scholarship.

Continuing as Scholar

While sub-warden at Merton College, Tolkien devoted himself to writing *The Homecoming of Beorhtnoth Beorhthelm's Son*, a straight play about the famous **epic** poem, *The Battle of Malden*, an historically true battle of the tenth century between the Vikings and the English. The fragment of the epic preserved today tells of the Vikings' demand for tribute money and Beorhtnoth's refusal which led to his valiant fighting and finally his death.

"The Lay of Aotrou and Itroun" appeared in 1945 and "Imram," in 1955. Both are narrative poems.

THE TRILOGY

"The Lord of the Rings"

1954 marked the publication of *The Fellowship of the Ring*, the first volume in Tolkien's trilogy, *The Lord of The Rings*. *The Two Towers*, the second volume, also appeared in the literary marketplace in 1954. The final volume, *The Return of the King*, followed in 1955. These represent creative expression in moments snatched from duty in true dedication to structuring another world. The massive work had, of course, been in progress for more than fourteen years but duties as a scholar, the Second World War, and other activities had delayed any early publication soon after *The Hobbit* of the thirties. Tolkien had, however, been spinning his yarn almost in the manner of the old teller of tales, presenting his work to the Inklings in an atmosphere of profound Christianity. A built-in understanding permitted the author great freedom in developing his **theme**. Other fiction which captured Tolkien's attention was *The Silmarillion* on which he was working at the time of his death.

Tolkien's professorial years, steeped in Anglo-Saxon language and literature, put their stamp on his work. Tolkien's exceptional familiarity with ancient lore rendered him able to fashion twentieth-century fiction in the manner of legend and myth. Tolkien belonged to the world of philologists, word lovers. With his particular gift for using words, he subcreated, from his vast wealth of learning, his intriguing Middle Earth, that fascinating Other World which is significantly related to our own.

The Lord of the Rings was written in long hand, an immense task at the outset. Revision, of course, followed and then the whole work was rewritten backward. The about-to-be famous novelist could not afford a typist so he typed up the three volumes himself - 600,000 words. This must have been a labor of love.

THE SIXTIES

Additional Publications

As fame came to the quiet, reserved Oxford don, he continued to focus on scholarly avenues. Tolkien became a principal collaborator in the gigantic task of translating and revising *The Jerusalem Bible*. Tolkien's province was writing an introduction to Job and translating that book which recounts the faith of a resolute man severely tried by his God.

The Sixties brought more honors and more work. The Royal Society of Literature presented Tolkien with the Benson Medal. In 1961 Tolkien proved himself a master of **parody** with the publication of *The Adventures of Tom Bombadil*. Philology and literary scholarship were his targets. Tolkien, familiar with two collections of ancient Welsh poetry, *The Black Book of Carmarthen* and the *Red Book of Hergst*, used these two sources as models for his Red Book of West March, which, he announced at this point, contained verse. These poems constitute *The Adventures of Tom Bombadil*. Hobbits, he claimed, had written these doggerel-like poems which range from narratives like Tom's courting of Goldberry to the nonsense-type nursery **rhyme**, "The Man in the Moon Stayed Up Too Late" and the "Fastitocalon," parodying the ancient sea beast of the scholars.

The Tolkien Reader appeared in 1966, containing reprints of "*The Homecoming of Beorhtnoth Beorhtelm's Son*," "*Tree and Leaf*," which was originally the Andrew Lang Lecture "*On Fairy*

Stories," "Farmer Giles of Ham," and "The Adventures of Tom Bombadil," as well as an introduction by Peter Beagle, "*Tolkien's Magic Ring.*" 1967 brought Tolkien fans another charming fantasy, Smith of Wootton Major, a light, humorous piece dealing with a bit of Elven magic in a birthday cake. *The Road Goes Ever On: A Song Cycle* joined the list of Tolkien's published works in 1968. This contained lyrics by the author set to compositions by Donald Swain.

Tolkien never lost sight of scholarly pursuits. In 1969 he translated *The Pearl* (circa 1370), a poetic **elegy** dealing with the death of a small girl and expounding the doctrine of grace according to St. Augustine. He also reaffirmed his continuing interest in the Middle Ages with a translation of *Sir Gawain and the Green Knight*, the verse romance which he had edited as one of his first published works back in 1925.

RETIREMENT YEARS

Work at Home

By the time the don doffed his cap and gown, the traditional serenity of the university town of Oxford was giving way to technology with a higher population in the colleges and an increase in traffic on the once-quiet streets. The professor's reticence about his own personal life continued to the end, despite his literary stature. He always harbored a persistent distaste for being written about in publications. He refused permission to be considered in Contemporary Writers in Christian Perspective published by Erdsman. The unassuming, wispy-haired man, gentle and shy by nature, could become noticeably truculent in his persistent endeavors to escape the public eye.

Tolkien enjoyed only a short period of retirement. His last days he busily devoted to *The Silmarillion*, a prequel to his famous trilogy. At Headington Hill, a little street near the London Road in Oxford, Tolkien lived in a three-bedroom house with a back garden fence which he had built himself. Tolkien worked in his study in the garage, in addition to doing a lot of household tasks because of his wife's illness. W. H. Auden considered the house hideous. He said, "I can't tell you how awful it is - with hideous pictures on the wall."

Books filled the study. It also contained a powder horn which Tolkien cherished as well as a very, very old portmanteau given him by his guardian. A map of Middle Earth of course added an appropriate touch.

When questioned about the delay in the publication of *The Silmarillion*, the author described this work as "exhausting." "God help us, yes. Most of the time I'm fighting against the natural inertia of the lazy human being." The novel actually is said to have been written before the trilogy but was rejected by a publisher. Now greatly in demand, the book has never been published.

Tolkien died in September, 1973, at the age of eighty-one, having intriguingly revived the ancient uses of myth, **epic**, and romance for twentieth-century readers.

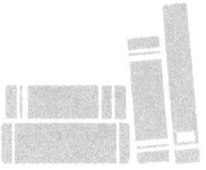

THE FELLOWSHIP OF THE RING

TEXTUAL ANALYSIS

THEMES AND TECHNIQUES IN "THE FELLOWSHIP OF THE RING"

MAJOR THEMES

The overriding twin **themes** of *The Fellowship of the Ring* stand like two armies in conflict, their abstractions brought alive by a variety of literary techniques. The textual analysis has revealed the doom-filled power of the One Ring which triggers off the mission of the Fellowship of the Nine, their goal being the destruction of the demonic trinket. The story vibrates with the struggle between life and death forces. Tolkien expresses his beliefs about absolutes and verities which add considerable depth to what otherwise might be merely a "tall tale."

The author sees two forces at work in his Middle Earth-evil and good. These two major forces form umbrellas for a number of related themes. Life and death, evil and good are in combat.

RELATED THEMES

Power of Evil

In the struggle between life-forces which represent good and death forces which represent evil, the power of evil in *The Fellowship of the Ring* appears to exceed that of good. Evil seems to have an edge on the agents for right against wrong. Evil's strength lies in its all-pervasiveness whereas good seems to emerge as a sporadic bright spot here and there on a black canvas.

In this novel the One Ring hastily reduces a splendid character like Bilbo or Frodo to the depraved level of the enemy itself. The power of the ring crushes individuality and stretches a person so thin that he merely exists instead of lives. The effects of evil spread out endlessly; man can never recover totally from confrontation with depravity. Evil manifests itself in a strong determination to dominate. Selfishness is its core.

Man's Responsibility for His Actions

Man (or hobbit) possesses free will which enables him to act independently according to the dictates of his own conscience. No matter how seemingly inadequate he is, an individual somehow is able to find courage within himself when he is responding to duty as his inner voice directs him, even to the point of great sacrifice. The passage from immaturity to manhood removes man from his initial state of innocence which is fraught with danger because of its lack of suspicion and guile. Innocence leaves man open to the clutches of evil.

A corollary to the concept of man's being responsible for his actions focuses on the notion of the elect. An overall purpose in a universal plan selects one individual to carry out a mission. This concept rules out the element of chance and explains at least in part the remarkable ability to endure which comes to one who is summoned to do a task that is seemingly beyond his capabilities.

Love

Love tends to humanize the effects of evil in the world. Power against evil exists in union as in the Fellowship in which breeds of creatures dissolve their differences and bend their efforts toward a common goal. Man's love for his fellowman in Tolkien's view follows the idealized Greek pattern for love and friendship between two men. Love also takes another form here - that of hero worship. Man reveres his leader. Maternal and paternal types of love serve as instruments of protection and concern for the general well being of the community and especially the weaker individuals in need of help. Love between the sexes wears as thick coat of idealization and romance. This affection takes a second-rate spot in contrast to the examples of manly devotion.

Time

Unusual concepts about time occur in *The Fellowship of the Ring*. Chronological time forms the basis for narration and contributes objectivity. But time also emerges as an element to be reckoned with. It is the enemy of the good. Pressures of time running out before good forces can triumph creates tension and hostility. The second hand moves inexorably and dangerously fast in areas where man (or hobbit) finds himself threatened.

On the other hand, a timelessness without seconds, minutes, hours, or even days infiltrates the idyllic havens of safety, suggesting the pleasant, paradisiacal elements in the cocoon of everlasting life. Such a sense of immortality as this timelessness gives relates to the serene implication of an overall purpose in the universe, no matter how much chaos may seem to reign. The Christian concept of a well-ordered cosmos with one God in charge of all remains implicit throughout the work, though in no way does Tolkien even overtly refer to any orthodox religion.

Waste Lands

Tolkien uses the notion of devastation to prove the arid results of evil on earth. Lands lie withered and barren, robbed of their natural bloom and health by wicked creatures. Areas that once boasted fairness have now turned into darkness. Trees stand leafless, stark and dead. A sinful night throws shadows over the world. Pestilence and war have laid waste the earth, indicating the decadence of civilization. Man's technology has emerged as his enemy in a materialistic world.

Soil

Whatever is benevolent, whatever is kind, must be closely associated with the soil, according to Tolkien's view. Human relations flourish in a rural, bucolic atmosphere. This promotes marriage, family life, happy childhoods and contented adulthoods with a sense of fulfillment of one's own worth as an individual. The agrarian type society emerges as desirable for the expression of individuality. Nature fosters the fullest type of self-realization.

On the other hand the dangers of complacency may occur, lulling one into a somnolent apathy toward the upsurge of evil in the world. Another caveat which Tolkien issues concerns the related danger of isolationism; that is, surrounding one's self and one's community with a literal or figurative wall. Living like an island severs man from his responsibility to war against evil at all times.

Tolkien believes that men should possess inalienable rights as individuals to live peaceful and harmonious lives. Constant vigilance against an infringement on these rights demands that man serve as a responsible protector.

Corruption

Tolkien views the world and people (or hobbits) as dangerously susceptible to corruption through the agents of evil. Evil, he believes, is good distorted. All evil had its origin in good like the fallen angels. The essence of depravity blights benevolence but only if weakness permits the wicked agent to triumph. The only real weapon against corruption rests in inner resources and strength.

LITERARY TECHNIQUES AND STYLE

Point of View

Tolkien writes as the omniscient author, knowing all things about Middle Earth and its creatures. He claims to have drawn his materials mainly from the *Red Book of Westmarch*, a chronicle of events at the end of the Third Age and the War of the Ring. The diaries of Bilbo and Frodo Baggins form the basis for the Red Book. Thus, Tolkien slyly abdicates his role as creator of the material. He writes in the third person.

The omniscient author's ability to select information which he wants to convey allows him the freedom to live in Frodo's mind quite often, expressing fears and sorrows. Subjective treatment of emotions by seeing into the heart of the little hobbit slants the novel toward revealing Frodo's point of view. Second to this, Sam Gamgee's emotions become clear when on occasion the author visits inside the faithful servant.

These two perspectives illuminate the reader as to how these characters think and feel, thereby permitting the reader to identify with the two survivors of the Fellowship who will make the journey to Mordor. Also insight into Frodo's thoughts and emotions assist Tolkien in presenting his themes about the development of courage in time of need and the special designation of one individual for a big task. Knowledge of Sam's innermost reactions provides additional reader-identification because Sam is "one of us," an ordinary, undistinguished little creature in the midst of overpowering challenges.

Narration

Narration in *The Fellowship of the Ring* evidences Tolkien's unique gifts as an author. Several types move the story along at varying speeds. Certain characters, generally prominent personages, deliver long monologues for the purpose of edifying both the reader and other characters about history, creatures of the supernatural world, and the ring. These monologues possess a fairy-tale quality as surely as if they began. "Once upon a time." And sometimes they seem to, as subjects and events frequently have occurred in the far-distant past.

Injections of different types of poetry provide another Tolkienesque touch. The quality of the poetry, on the whole, lacks distinction and cannot well exist outside the text as a poetic entity. The tone contributes to the mood of the scene in the case of little poems like Bilbo's farewell song or the hobbit's bath song. Long lays like the tale of Tinuviel show the influence of medieval writings on Tolkien who uses the term annthennath from the Elven tongue to describe these sentimentalized, narrative poems.

A third type of narrative which Tolkien employs is straight storytelling about the travels of the ringbearer and his companions, complete with the usually brief exchanges of dialogue common to contemporary fiction.

Symbolism

Symbolism as a vehicle for reinforcing **themes** follows tradition with Tolkien. The use of black to signify evil even extends to the shadow encompassing Middle Earth. Supernatural creatures like orcs and ring-wraiths appear clothed in black. Waste lands, the decaying cities and widespread, arid areas, equate the decadence of civilization because of evil. Cold also suggests depravity. Trees represent life as does the flourishing natural world populated by certain creatures like the Elves who are agents of good. Flowers, both Elvish and familiar, function for the good. White raiment signifies the purity of those wearing it.

Tolkien has created the hobbit to be Everyman. The passage from the "tweens" to adulthood symbolizes his development into a responsible individual. Crossing a body of water, like baptismal rites, shows development also, either that of the individual moving toward greater strength or that of the fellowship's encountering new challenges. Frodo's extraordinary wounds demonstrate the scar tissue which evil leaves on its recipient.

Fire acts as an illuminating, purifying element. Inscription on the One Ring can be read only when it is heated in flames and it can be destroyed only by being tossed into the Fire of Doom in which it was forged. The One Ring, the supreme symbol of evil, can encircle the whole earth.

Allegory

Steeped in symbolism, *The Fellowship of the Ring*, as a story which contains a deeper meaning than appears in the plot, may be termed an allegory. It reveals the age-old struggle of man (or hobbit), an agent for good, fighting against the forces of evil. Considered as an allegory, the novel puts forth universalities commonly found in this type of literature-the long-suffering, persistent **protagonist** trying to save the world and himself as well against a powerful adversary. The supernatural world here divides into two bands-one for food and one for evil.

Fantasy and Verity Techniques

Tolkien's use of **realism**, picturing in literature things as they actually are, strikes an unusual note since he is dealing with the world of Faerie. Such **realism** increases the reader's credulity. Even in the company of supernatural creatures, commonplace items of food appear on the table along with magical drinks. Although fantastic characters may wear shimmering robes, the hobbits appear in the human-type clothing, albeit in especially bright colors. (Their hairy feet, however, need no shoes.)

Gwaihir, king of the Eagles of the Misty Mountains, and Shadowfax, the silvery steed with the fleetest of feet, move in the same world as Sam's beloved old nag, Bill. The juxtaposition of realistic and fantastic elements offers stimulating contrasts.

The use of verity techniques extends to the characters. No matter how supernatural the literary personages may be, they do not lose their humanity. They, in fact, exaggerate it extravagantly. The agents for good carry benevolence to superhuman lengths in their magnificent bounty. Reversely, the agents for evil encompass the quintessence of depravity. The reader, however, goes along easily with the extremes because the techniques in this type of presentation make use of familiar personality traits or clothing and induce believability.

Humor

Tolkien has the ability to make the reader chuckle from time to time. Humor occurs largely in the informal scenes and possesses a gentleness which is welcome amid much high tension, induced by danger and imminent doom. Tolkien's comicality arises from his capitalizing on the human qualities of especially the hobbits. Their foibles and weaknesses like those of the average little man emerge as ludicrous reminders of the very humanity of those undertaking a gigantic, hero-type task. The ridiculous effects of hobbits' trembling amid dangers stems from an incongruity that so human a creature could be thrust into the august company of kings and rulers and into the pits of evil and doom.

Comments on society also contain humor. For example, the social-climbing Sackville-Bagginses (the S. - B.'s, so called) present a funny case of the modified avarice of gentility, blatant within limits but foiled to a degree by Bilbo's wit.

Historical Allusions

The Fellowship of the Ring contains historical **allusions** of two types. Certain **allusions** form stories in themselves as in the case of Gandalf's narrative to Frodo about the One Ring - how it came into being and its history of being captured from *Sauron* by Isildur son of Elendil and his subsequent loss of the magic token. Other **allusions** resemble long recitatives in verse as in Bilbo's chant about Earendil, the mariner. Both fill the reader (and the immediate audience as well) with information pertinent to the story of the ring. Occasionally the author himself provides a historical passage as in the explanation of the Brandybuck family in the area in which Frodo purported to be moving from Bag End in the Shire. *The Book of Marzbul*, discovered by the company on its journey through Khazad-Dum, the folkhome and mansion of the dwarfs, supplies the history of those creatures. These different methods of referring to history all serve the purpose of giving multiple details about Tolkien's secondary world and its inhabitants.

Description and Diction

One cannot read Tolkien's works without being impressed with his love affair with language. Evidence of this occurs in several ways - in his use of unusual and archaic words, in his invention of the Elven tongue and in the bevy of well-chosen adjectives to describe landscapes and picturesque dwellings. Wold, fen and tussock, eyot, wind-writhen, to choose only a few examples, pepper the pages, refreshing the reader with variations from the commonplace. Gandalf's spectacular fireworks with, for one item, green rees - "their leaves opened like a whole spring unfolding at once." "... farm buildings peeping out among the trees ahead," "... a fair young elf-queen clad in living flowers ..." "The young Sun shown like fire on the red metal of their new and greedy swords ..." "... standing stones, pointing upwards like jagged teeth out of green gums" all show Tolkien's ability to paint beautiful pictures. He does not lack talent in describing the demonic though at times he wisely elects to leave details to the reader's imagination. As for the monstrous Balrog, scant information appears - "and the shadow about it reached out like two vast wings." "Fire came from its nostrils." "It raised its whip, and the thing whined and cracked." Frodo' black robed assailants had "white faces" in which "burned keen and merciless eyes.

Space affords only a sprinkling of the unique geographical names. Ettenmoors, the Dimrill Stair, Mordor, Khazad-Dum, Lothlorien all attest the author's love of sound as well as his exceptional ability to make up appropriate words which give the nature of the landscape. The names of the characters - Frodo, Gandalf, Boromir, Elendil - the list could go on endlessly - have no connection with the commonplace except for Sam whose name was deliberately chosen to signify a down-to-earth, humble gardener.

Tolkien shows his hand at doing nonsense-verse in the **parody** on the nursery **rhyme** "Hey diddle diddle, the cat and the fiddle" and in Tom Bombadil's songs with "derry dol" and "ring a ding dillo."

The author's forte of inventing languages reveals itself especially in the Eleven tongue in which he comes up with short phrases like "'Elen sila lumenn omentilmo,'" which Frodo translates as "a star shines on the hour of our meeting." Beyond that Tolkien composes an entire song which Arwen And Aragorn sing to Elbereth, worshipped by the Elves.

Tolkien's style of writing both in narrative passages and dialogue tends toward the stilted archaic either by choice of words of arrangement. For example, "... he left the hill of Cerin Amroth and came there never again as living man." Lady Galadriel's speech features inverted sentences, "Dark is the water of Kheled-zaram, and cold are the springs of Kibil-nala, and fair were the many pillared halls of Khazad-Dum in Elder Days before the fall of mighty kings beneath the stone." Proverb-type statements also show archaic touches. "Faithless is he that says farewell when the road darkens." But, all in all, the quaint words and wordings really enhance the atmosphere of the ancient days which Tolkien set out to create.

Contrasts and Parallels

Tolkien thrives on extremes. His contrasts offer incredibly wide dichotomy while at the same time bringing up parallels of much the same cloth. Frodo with the core of goodness and selflessness in his heart differs strikingly from his adversary, Gollum, distorted by constant association with the evil ring. Two ruling figures remain at opposite ends of the spectrum between morality and depravity. Aragorn, whom the reader comes to recognize as a king aspiring to claim his throne, possesses the traditional attributes of a King Arthur type ruler - goodness, high standards, courage, physical stamina. Sauron, his unseen opponent, incarnates evil itself. The same striking contrast exists between Gandalf and the Balrog monster which pulls the wizard into the abyss. Again the elements of good vie with the elements of evil. Among the supernatural creatures the star-blessed Elves emanate love and protectiveness whereas the dreadful orcs wear the blackness of wickedness and sin.

Paralleling the Elves as guardians of the hobbits, Tom Bombadil and Goldberry embody goodness. Tom, in fact, being of nature, stands above the power of the ring. Goldberry, too, suggests natural forces in the purest form. Enormous similarity exists between the two Elven ladies, Arwen and Galadriel. Both possess outstanding beauty and both attract great love. Their roles reveal them as royal ladies in the traditional strain, lovely, kind, lofty, above reproach. Similar stereotypes exist in the two Elven male rulers, Celeborn and Elrond. Celeborn ruled justly in Lorein and fought bravely against Sauron in the battle of Dol Guldur. Also a just ruler in Imladris, Elrond through his wisdom and knowledge aided the forces fighting evil. By presenting contrasts and parallels, Tolkien offers his readers variety held well in harness by a sense of balance.

Personification

The author embodies his abstract elements in order to strengthen the **themes** and, in addition, he uses personification most effectively in his description of objects in nature. Sauron the Dark Ruler and his underlings, the nine ringwraiths and the black orcs, give the reader a picture of depravity in person. Tom Bombadil, lord and master of the Old Forest, or better still, its steward, embodies a clear, untrammeled natural spirit. While other characters like Gollum or Gandalf possess undeniable abstract traits, their individualization as creatures lifts them above the level of mere personification.

Tolkien skillfully personifies object in nature, perhaps none better than the three mountains, especially Caradhras which attacks the hobbits with a snowstorm. Old Man Willow, trying to capture the hobbits, resembles a Disney cartoon.

Metaphor, Simile and Imagery

The figures of speech, **metaphor, simile**, and **imagery**, enable Tolkien to furnish imaginative pictures for his reader to visualize all the more clearly the person or objects described. **Metaphor** refers to one thing as if it were another. **Simile** likens one object to another. **Imagery** produces mental images. These devices tie in closely with the author's heavy dependence on symbolism. As Bilbo mysteriously leaves the Shire, the soft-stepping hobbit vanishes through the hedge "like a rustle of wind in the grass." The ring is described varyingly as a great weight to the one it would enthrall, and sometimes like an eye, an all-seeing eye. The transforming power of the ring manifests itself in Boromir - "the strange gleam in Boromir's eyes," "a raging fire in his eyes." Gandalf, in fencing off the wolves with fire, emerges "a great menacing shape like the monument of some ancient king of stone set upon a hill." In the blinding snowstorm Frodo's feet "felt like lead."

Tolkien excels in passages on the beautiful as in the house of Tom Bombadil where Tom dresses for dinner "all in clean blue, blue as rain-washed forget-me-nots." And Goldberry "held a candle, shielding its flame from the drought with her hand; and the light flowed through it, like sunlight through a white shell." The Elves evoke lovely images. "They bore no lights, yet as they walked a shimmer, like the light of the moon above the rim of the hills before it rises, seemed to fall about their feet."

Elements in nature stand sharply vivid as, for example, in the description of the great snow drift. "It was flung across the mountain path like a sheer and sudden wall, and its crest, sharp as if shaped with knives, reared up ..." In the Old Forest the hobbits find "a green hill-top rising like a bald head out of the encircling wood." Old Man Willow has "great winding roots ... like gnarled dragonets straining down to drink" from the water. These few examples demonstrate Tolkien's deftness in the use of descriptive figures of speech to add vitality to characters and scenes.

Summary Of Criticism Of Style

Tolkien offers the reader a literary style totally his own, yet rich in tradition. As evidenced in the examples, his choice of words contains a freshness with an archaic flavor. His invention of languages attesting to his originality adds a uniqueness seldom found in contemporary literature.

Tolkien, in fact, stands out among modern authors as a writer in the medieval tradition. Most of his sentences are so exceedingly long that the majority of today's novelists would quail at trying to employ them successfully. But, because of the appropriateness, Tolkien can use length when brevity is really the fashion of the day.

The same is true of scenes. The thirty-three page chapter, "The Council of Elrond," contains a scene in the ruler's chambers incredibly long in the market place of contemporary fiction. Within this chapter as well as throughout the book, characters speak at great length, narrating history and stories which, while somewhat entities in themselves, also belong to the great tapestry of the secondary world which Tolkien is creating. The use of poetry proves another daring addition. Who but Tolkien would scatter verses and lays throughout a basically prose work?

For the literary style of *The Fellowship of the Ring* Tolkien has absorbed much of medieval literature and yet he has presented a work sparkling with his own inventiveness and originality.

Tolkien Formula For Fiction

Tolkien weaves his fictional pattern out of fantasy, **epic** and myth. Fantasy for this highly imaginative author relates to an invented secondary world with its own well-ordered system of operation. The spectacular mingles with the real and the ordinary in Tolkien's imagined world; employing this method achieves the necessary credibility on the part of the reader. While wizards and elves and orcs inhabit the regions of fantasy so indeed do horses, birds, men, moons, suns, and familiar skies. Fantasy depends on portions of the real world to give substance to its airiness. Hobbits represent the author's real coup in this area.

Oddly enough, a strong relationship exists between fantasy and comedy, the two literary **genres** being close kin. Fantasy allows the author to express his own sense of the irrationality alive in the world. In the case of Tolkien, evil forces create chaos on all sides. But different from most fantasies which often take the form of **burlesque**, as in Eugene Ionesco's *Rhinoceros*, this novel has deadly serious surface atmosphere as well as an underlying solemnity of theme.

The high seriousness of *The Fellowship of the Ring* and the noble purpose of the ridiculously small band of the ringbearer land this work in the area of the **epic** also. Epics traditionally lean toward dignity; in the overall picture of Tolkien's trilogy dignity prevails although hobbits on occasion frolic a bit.

Beginning in the middle also characterizes the **epic** form.

Breadth and amplitude also typify this **genre**. Certainly Tolkien provides these requisites when he panoramically encompasses the entire Middle Earth. **Epics** generally possess a unifying series of events somehow causally related. The whole work remains unsettled to the end. *The Fellowship of the Ring* leaves the reader on a high note of suspense, awaiting fulfillment in the sequels. If **epics** must reflect the feeling and thought of people living in the author's time, Tolkien must speak for the disenchanted in the contemporary world who feel the shadow of wars and technology spreading over what might hopefully be a simpler and a better world.

While Frodo *The Hobbit* stands out as the leading figure in the trilogy, Tolkien's work does possess characters of **epic** proportion as in Aragorn, a traditional type hero, a superior and honorable being of a princely class. He transcends lowly interests. According to early traditions of less sophisticated societies, he makes no sharp distinction between what tasks he performs. Manual and martial duties alike fall under his obligations. In addition to fantasy and **epic**, elements of myth enrich Tolkien's work, a myth all of his own, a vast mixture of resources from Norse sagas and other Germanic lore. Myth extends **metaphor** and dramatizes symbolical, fictional speculations on the origin and purpose of man and nature. (Tolkien also makes use of legends, stories popularly believed with probably no verifiable basis in history; this is not to be confused with myth.) Myth with Tolkien endeavors to explain natural phenomena and describe the human condition. Traditional mythologies tend to personify elements in the natural world; Tolkien fabricates his own to personify the abstract forces with which man must contend. Tolkien's secondary world appears more like a Valhalla or Olympia because of his cosmic approach to man's world.

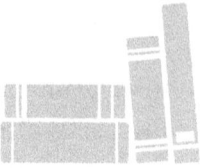

THE FELLOWSHIP OF THE RING

TEXTUAL ANALYSIS

PART 1

PROLOGUE AND NOTE ON SHIRE RECORDS

Literary Style

The Prologue constitutes an expository essay with encyclopaedic details about hobbits, creatures of the author's imagination. Straightforward explanations describe the red-cheeked creatures two to four feet tall, dressed in bright-colored clothing without shoes because of their leathery soled feet covered with curling hair. A gentleness overshadows the strictly objective point of view, reflecting the author's affection for the fanciful creatures.

Words from hobbit language bring unique touches to the writing. Smial, for example, means the big, rambling tunnels in which hobbits live. Mathoms designate any useless things which hobbits are unwilling to throw away. The sounds of names which Tolkiens gives to people and places ring strange notes: Harfoots, Stoors, and Fallohides represent the three different breeds of hobbits. Bilbo Baggins and his nephew, Frodo, principal characters of the trilogy, *The Lord of the Rings*, both possess uncommon first names as do many of the Tooks and Brandybucks who populate the Shire. Bluntness in the masculine-sounding names suggests a flavor of Anglo-Saxonism.

Content

The Prologue points out hobbits' pride in genealogical records, their delight in large families, and their enjoyment of pipe weed. Its purpose, revealing recent history necessary for understanding the novel, differs from that of Geoffrey Chaucer in *The Canterbury Tales* where the Prologue serves only to introduce characters who will tell tales. The sociological nature of this report gives the reader enough knowledge for him to be at ease in the fantasy.

The hobbits' Shire calls to mind idyllic communities in literature. It parallels Sir Thomas More's *Utopia* where the government-ruled family forms the basic unit of the state. Like the inhabitants of another Utopian novel. *Erewhon* by Samuel Butler, hobbits distrust machines. Tolkien's anti-technological views resemble those of Erich Fromm who cautions against the "reification" of modern man. A similar disciple, Herbert Marcuse, regards today's human being as a One Dimensional Man and protests against technological inhumanity.

As an alternative to this evil, Tolkien summons up visions of a medieval community where life centered around the castle of a benevolent lord who protected his people from dire dangers beyond the boundaries. The Took family has claimed the title of Thain of the hobbits for many generations, the top governing post. Bounders resemble fortress guards who watch for danger in the countryside and sound an ominous note of peril to the peaceful Shire. The community, with its jolly tavern, tunnel-type abodes, and neat gardens sustains an entity similar to manor life of the Middle Ages.

Nature of Subject Matter

Tolkien employs fantasy, adroitly setting his story in far-distant times and presenting precise details about this imagined world. Its creatures-orcs, dwarves, elves, and hobbits-behave like human beings. Historical details about the Dark Plague and the Days of Dearth and the Battle of Greenfields against invading orcs have an air of authenticity. An actual map shows the area bounded by the Gulf of Lune, the Iron Hills, the Bay of Forochel, and the River Anduin.

Tolkien follows his own dictum for the fairy story as he set it forth in his essay, "On Fairy-Stories" - "it should be presented as 'true.'" In creating fantasy, "What really happens is that the story-maker proves a successful 'sub-creator.' He makes a Secondary World which your mind can enter. Inside it, what he relates is 'true': it accords with the laws of the world. You therefore believe it, while you are, as it were, inside." Samuel Taylor Coleridge, the eminent British poet and critic who wrote considerably about the uses of imagination in literature, called this "the willing suspension of disbelief."

The author owes a debt to Richard Wagner for the major fantastic element of *The Fellowship of the Ring*, the One Ring itself. The Wagnerian operatic cycle, The Nibelungenlied, turns on a ring of the Rhinedaughters' gold which makes the owner all-powerful. Tolkien's ring, also bestowing power, can, in addition, make the wearer invisible and virtually ageless.

Themes Introduced

The ring communicates Tolkien's major **theme** concerning the struggle between evil and good. In the combat the survival of spirit as a life-giving force signifies an emphasis on man's inner resources. The author will more sharply identify the characteristics of evil and good as the story develops. Bilbo, the hobbit found the ring, thereby introducing another theme-the element of chance versus the doctrine of the elect, the one chosen by plan to execute a mission. This implies the author's underlying belief in a purposeful, guided universe.

Symbolism

Tolkien's use of symbolism reinforces his message. The ring represents power and avarice. Hobbits are the innocent of mankind-small, child-like creatures who inhabit tunnel-type dwellings. Bilbo's smial, Bag End, suggests the womb. The round door "opened on a tube-shaped hall like a tunnel," which may be interpreted as the vagina. When Bilbo leaves Bag End, he is born into the world of experience and confrontation with evil.

Time and Timelessness

At the outset the reader becomes involved with several aspects of time-in the timelessness of antiquity and different methods of reckoning time. Shire-reckoning, the calendar system of the Shire, commences with the year 1601 of the Third Age which was the Shire year One. Within this framework the usual chronological concept of time functions. Early evidence of Tolkien's preference for chronological sequence in narration appears in the Prologue's section on Bilbo's experience "Of Finding the Ring." This section also introduces the ever-present concept of time as the enemy of the good forces. Time almost runs out on Bilbo in his efforts to escape Gollum, hobbit-turned-monster in the dark orc mines under the mountain.

Structure of Bilbo's Story

The mini-story of Bilbo's finding the ring, condensing Tolkien's first novel, *The Hobbit*, opens with a conventional introduction giving way immediately to rising action. After Bilbo has found the ring, the **climax** is a contest between Bilbo and Gollum. Like the question and answer session between Mime and the disguised Wotan in Wagner's Siegfried, wit proves to be Bilbo's salvation. The struggle contains an element of pity when Bilbo refuses to kill the monster. The **denouement** brings an end to Bilbo's adventures as he settles down at Bag End with his sword, Sting, over the fireplace and his magic mail given him by the dwarves in the local museum. This indicates that Tolkien will follow a traditional narrative pattern in the trilogy, *The Lord of the Rings*.

Note on Shire Records

The Note pinpoints the historical sources for the forthcoming story, the most important being the *Red Book of Westmarch*, which provided the author with the necessary history. This method harks back to that of Chretien de Troyes, the twelfth-century chronicler who claimed that his *Le Conte de Graal* or *Roman de Perceval* stemmed from a book of his patron, Philippe d'Alsace. This method adds authenticity. Most medieval authors employed some variation of this method of pretending to be retelling a tale.

CHAPTER 1, BOOK I: A LONG EXPECTED PARTY

Chapter 1 is actually another prologue, presenting preliminary events leading up to the main narrative in which the fellowship begins.

Literary Style

The manner of writing departs strikingly from that of the Prologue, using dialogue and poetry. Dialogue informs the reader about Bilbo's seemingly enormous wealth, his apparently eternal youth, and his intention to leave the Shire. It establishes Gandalf's relationship with both Bilbo and Frodo and Frodo's possession of the magic ring.

For the first time poetry, an integral part of Tolkien's style, appears. Hobbits burst into song to indicate their state of mind, thereby heightening the mood of a scene. As Bilbo starts his great adventure, strangely compelled to join the dwarves again after many years at Bag Eng, he sings his song of the Road. The line, "Pursuing it with eager feet," depicts his joy at entering the unknown.

Subjective description now replaces factual reports. The Shire possesses bucolic beauty with the flowers in Bilbo's garden glowing "red and golden," snap-dragons, sunflowers, and nasturtiums 'trailing all over the turf walls and peeping in at the round windows." Notice the use of personification in the latter image. The spectacular fireworks resemble pictures in the sky - "rockets like a flight of scintillating birds singing with sweet voices." Tolkien scores well with briefer passages like Bilbo's description of the ring. "'Sometimes I have felt it was like an eye looking at me.'" The hobbit's departure from the Shire into the night is "like a rustle of wind in the grass." Gandalf describes the angry Lobelia Sackville-Baggins with "'a face that would have curdled new milk.'" Notice that the last three images are similes: figures of speech that overtly express a likeness between unlike things with a word like or as.

Numbers

The use of numbers in Hobbiton demonstrates Tolkien's originality. On his birthday Bilbo becomes eleventh-one, "a very respectable age for a hobbit." Frodo, Bilbo's adopted nephew, is coincidentally thirty-three on the same day. This anniversary marks a hobbit's coming of age. Frodo passes out of his tweens, "the irresponsible twenties between childhood and coming of age at thirty three." Bilbo calls the 144 birthday party guests "one gross," insulting some who do not relish being compared to packaged goods.

Humor

"Gross" exemplifies the gentle humor which Tolkien sprinkles through this homey chapter. The reader can chuckle over the gossip about the death of Frodo's parents in the Brandywine River. Bilbo's farewell speech causes such restlessness and boredom that some youngsters start an impromptu orchestra while some dance the Springle-ring. Shock so great grips the guests at Bilbo's disappearance that they must have more food and drink. Gardeners remove in wheel barrows "those that had inadvertently remained behind." Absurd behavior continues as three hobbits knock holes in Frodo's cellar walls and another starts excavating for buried treasure.

Following the established hobbit custom of constant gift giving, Bilbo leaves behind appropriately selected presents. For example, Adelard Took receives an umbrella of his very own because he has made off with many others. Lobelia Sackville-Baggins, Bilbo's long-time adversary, gets a case of silver spoons because the donor suspects she has already taken a number of his.

Characterization

Having abandoned his encyclopaedic style, the author begins to personalize his characters, allowing them to speak for themselves. Frodo becomes master of Bag End, guarding his home against niggling scavengers. Bewilderment over owning the magic ring clutches *The Hobbit* grown to manhood as does the first glimmer of a feeling that he, too, will be leaving the Shire. The reader notes that at the advent of manhood Frodo is beginning to change.

Also, Frodo is an orphan. Leading figures in heroic literature frequently have unusual parental circumstances. Achilles, hero of Homer's *Iliad*, had one divine parent, Thetis, the sea nymph. While both of Frodo's parents were hobbits, they were of a queer breed living near the creepy Old Forest. His mother was a Brandybuck, not of a Shire family.

The introduction of Gandalf pigeonholes him at first as a commonplace wizard with his pointed hat and long cloak. Driving his cart full of magic firecrackers, he resembles a Pied

Piper amid clamoring children. Bilbo calls him "'an interfering old busybody,'" but the reader realizes that Gandalf represents a compendium of stock-in-trade tricks and ominous perceptions beyond mere human understanding. He exerts influence on Bilbo to leave the ring with Frodo and promises to look out for the new owner of the magic trinket, casting himself in the role of a mystical supervisor.

CHAPTER 2, BOOK I: THE SHADOW OF THE PAST

Chapter 2 is a crucial chapter in which Frodo Baggins undergoes his initiation into dangerous adventures.

Symbolism

The title, "The Shadow of the Past," suggests the image of evil from previous years which will resurface to bring darkness to the earth. Shadow also applies to dire sensations which Gandalf experiences in his heart when Bilbo acquires the ring. Gollum's preference for darkness marks him as evil, furthering the symbolic motif. In contrast, the fire, which makes the runes appear on the magic ring, foreshadows the trials which the fellowship will encounter, harking back to the experience of Shadrack, Meshach and Abednego who were cast into a furnace by Nebuchadnezzar. Tolkien uses symbolism to reinforce his themes.

Themes

The ring serves as a springboard for several themes. What the magic circle has done to Gollum and what it might have done to

Bilbo underscores one of Tolkien's most significant messages - power corrupts. A related warning emerges clearly in the tavern scene with the hobbits - the dangers of complacency. The little folks in their contented way shrug off forebodings of evil. The **theme** of the elect also comes to light here as Frodo deplores his role as ringbearer. "'I wish it had not happened in my time.'" "'Man's main responsibility,'" Gandalf replies, "'is to decide what to do with the time that he is given.'" Free will is implied.

Supernatural Elements

Tolkien writes naturally of the Tree Men, dwarves and Elves in his Third Age when supernatural creatures still inhabit the earth. Sauron, the black, powerful lord of the rings, is the personification of evil much in the manner of Lucifer or Satan in John Milton's *Paradise Lost*. Satan preferred guile to force in overcoming his enemy. Sauron, too, proves to be a master of deceit and treachery. Sauron, never seen in spite of being the title-giver of the trilogy, hovers in the background as a figure of stark evil. Another evil creature, Smeagol or Gollum, suggests the savage Caliban, son of the wicked sorceress, in *The Tempest* by Shakespeare. Both typify physical and emotional distortions from the norm.

The most intriguing supernatural properties belong to the ring. Gandalf explains a new dimension beyond its power to make the wearer invisible - a permanent fading of personality which can occur when an individual succumbs to the ring. It ultimately devours the individual. The ring also exerts power over the life force of the owner who does not die but exists in great weariness until he feels, as Bilbo did, "'thin and stretched.'" The ring produces a love-hate syndrome in anyone who falls prey to its mystical qualities.

Historical Allusions

References to past events fill the reader in with background information. Gandalf in lengthy narrative passages talks of the White Council who drove the dark power out of Mirkwood. He recalls the Battle of the Five Armies in which Thorin Oakenshield, the dwarf king, was killed. This is significant because afterward Bilbo and the party of dwarves were attacked by orcs. Bilbo subsequently lost his way and found the ring. Gandalf describes the heroes, Gil-galad, the Elven-king, and Elendil of Westernesse, who lost their lives overthrowing Sauron. He tells Frodo of Isildur, last owner of the ring before Gollum.

In addition to narrator, Gandalf functions as soothsayer, predicting immanent depravity in the form of Sauron. Like the soothsayer in Shakespeare's *Julius Caesar*, he warns Frodo to beware of the power of the ring but encourages the hobbit in the immense task of dethroning evil.

Autobiographical

Tolkien inserts bits of his life. The Shire resembles the gentle countryside where the author spent his boyhood near the forest which Shakespeare made memorable in *As You Like It*. Like Tolkien's village, the fictional area lies inland from the sea, a haven from dangers of the ocean.

Frodo's visions of mountains reflect the writer's desire to escape his busy routine. Tolkien seems to use Bilbo as his spokesman earlier in wanting peace and quiet. "'I might find somewhere I can finish my book,'" Bilbo says. Elven runes inscribed on the ring demonstrate Tolkien's expertise in ancient Scandinavian.

Since this novel was written just prior to World War II, a parallel between evil infiltrating Middle Earth and the spread of Nazism unavoidably exists, though Tolkien clearly denies any intention of relating to contemporary conditions.

CHAPTER 3, BOOK I: THREE IS COMPANY

The Fellowship

The title, "Three is Company," signifies the beginning of the formation of the fellowship of nine with Frodo, the ringbearer, Pippin (Peregrine Took) and Sam Gangee. Meaningful use of numbers suggests an inherent unity as in the Trinity. The fellowship will grow to nine, another mystical number revered by the Greeks. This parallels the numbering of the rings under the One Ring, three for the Elven-Kings and nine for men who became the Ringwraiths.

The fellowship reminds the reader of the Round Table of King Arthur. Old French romances designate the Round Table as the collective personality of Arthur's court. Sir Thomas Malory in *Le Morte Darthur* regarded the great military brotherhood of a royal household as a chivalric order. His chronicle has Guinevere's father present Arthur as a wedding gift the Round Table with one hundred knights. The popular Victorian version, *The Idylls of the King* by Alfred, Lord Tennyson, shows a strong king binding his knights to him with an oath in mystical ceremony.

While the fellowship of this novel contains a limited number, the practice of the Middle Ages of a unified band of military men fighting a common enemy prevails here.

Elements Of Adventure Story

The essential emphasis now rests on distance and space as opposed to the confines of the Shire. The trio, with packs aback, resembles a modern-day hiking group. Frodo quotes Bilbo's song of the road, suggesting an overall seriousness about this journey with destination unknown. The hobbits' initial encounter with a mysterious black rider forebodes danger and quixotic risk. The walking song about adventure heightens the atmosphere of anticipated excitement typical of adventure stories.

Characterization

Large and small additions in characterization appear here. After the Elven feast when Pippin, sound asleep, is carried to his tree bower, he resembles a little child. Childishness will characterize his later behavior. Sam, in refusing to leave his master although sleep overtakes him, demonstrates a faithfulness which calls to mind the squire of Don Quixote, Sancho Panza in Miguel de Cervantes Saavedra's novel *Don Quixote de la Mancha*. Sam appears to be a bucolic bumpkin like Sancho but, unlike the selfishly motivated squire, the hobbit gardener will prove to be an in-depth character.

Frodo remains very human, sad at leaving home. "'I wonder if I shall ever look down in the valley again.'" But he is already alert to danger at the sound of horses' hooves. A desire to protect himself makes him think of the ring. Yet he realizes that much will be demanded of him on his journey. He asks, "'Where shall I find courage? ... That is what I chiefly need.'"

The reader begins to sense in Frodo's character a certain sexlessness. Frodo had established himself as bachelor master of his womb-like home, Bag End. His very close relationship with Sam, Pippin and Merry indicates his preference for male companionship. This ties in significantly with Frodo's role as the ringbearer since he is apart from the average hobbit.

Star Motif

Starlight, which symbolizes good fortune, characterizes the Elven. "... the hobbits could see the starlight glimmering on their hair and in their eyes." Stars, ensigns of knightly rank, appropriately figure in their Ancient Tongue, an ingenious invention of the author which Frodo understands. "'Elen sila lumenn omentilmo,'" says Frodo. ("'A star shines on the hour of our meeting.'") Gildor Inglorion of the House of Finrod, leader of the Elves, both warns and blesses Frodo. "'The wide world is all about you: you can fence yourselves in, but you cannot forever fence it [danger] out.'" "'... may the stars shine upon the end of your road.'" Star worship of their queen, Elbereth, the Snow White, believed to have created the stars, constitutes the religion of these high-minded creatures and gives the author opportunity to suggest legends among ancient people like the Babylonians and even the Blackfoot Indians who believed that every star was once a human being.

CHAPTER 4, BOOK I: A SHORT CUT TO MUSHROOMS

The threatening Chapter 4 contrasts with the happy serenity of the Elves' company. Tolkien is establishing a pattern of pendulum-like movement in the interludes of the hobbits' journeys, going from frivolity to dark danger.

Characterization

As Frodo's suspicion that he has been elected ringbearer grows into the concept of an inheritance, his deep concern for his friends adds a Christlike dimension. Sam's Faithfulness to his master increases as does his sense of mission which he cannot yet identify. More importantly, a compulsion "'to take a very long road into darkness ...'" is leading Sam into the unknown.

Farmer Maggot functions as an informer, echoing the popular view of Bilbo as an eccentric with his gold and jewels buried in Hobbiton and revealing the black stranger's search for Frodo on the farmer's property. Maggot years ago had beaten Frodo for stealing mushrooms, dubbing him a thief which reinforces Frodo's role as a counter-part of Bilbo who was called "the burglar" on his expedition with the dwarves many years earlier. As protector providing the hobbits with a mighty supper of mushrooms and bacon and a wagon ride to the ferry in the evil-infested region, Farmer Maggot represents the goodness in those who love the soil and shelter the hobbits from harm.

Matter of Mushrooms

Frodo's extraordinary enjoyment of mushrooms opens a wide area of symbolic speculation. The ancient Greeks and Romans regarded mushrooms as highly prized delicacies, food of the gods. Traditionally this unusual plant had been associated with Mother Earth, the embodiment of fertility, goodness and health. But mushrooms frequently symbolize anything ephemeral or brieflived because of their rapid growing habits and swift decay. Mushrooms actually cause fairy rings. Circles of lighter grass result from mushrooms spawn which cannot grow long in one place. The grass above the spawn is thin at first but, as the spawn decays, it fertilizes the soil, producing thicker grass.

Complementing the symbolic spectrum offered by the capped fungi, maggot in rare usage refers to whims and fancies. More commonly maggot suggests filth and decay, emphasizing Tolkien's concern for the blight upon the world.

Descriptive Language

A variety of descriptions adorns this chapter. Pastoral qualities characterize passages about life with the Elves, like Frodo's bower and the Elves' magic drink. Description personalizes the landscape, a device which Tolkien favors. "... the bushes and brambles were reluctant to let them through." Hostile notes also figure in presenting mysterious cries - "A long drawn wail ... answered by another cry ... no less chilling to the blood." Harsh sounds typify the names of Farmer Maggot's fierce dogs, Grip, Fang, and Wolf. Masculine, abrupt, one-syllable names fit well the watchdogs who guard against the outside world. Inside the home a typical rural kitchen, well lit with candles and warmed by fires, welcomes the hobbits.

CHAPTER 5, BOOK I: A CONSPIRACY UNMASKED

Title

Tolkien suggests in the title that two or more of the characters have agreed to do something illegal or criminal. The author is having a little joke because his conspiracy involves three high-minded hobbits who will support Frodo in his struggle to conquer evil.

Historical Allusions

Tolkien's special gift in creating the Other World of Middle Earth relies on detailed though fake history which gives realistic substance to his fantasy. The area into which Frodo is moving, reportedly to a permanent home away from the Shire, was founded by Gorhendad Oldbuck. Having changed his name to Brandybuck, this notable pioneer built Brandy Hall, forming a hobbit community which enjoyed boating and swimming, diversions frowned on by Shire hobbits. Protecting, the community with its chief village of Buckleberry was the High Hay, a well tended, thick hedge twenty miles long, closing out the fearful Old Forest.

The community, comparatively isolated, resembles a medieval manor. The thriving, interdependent people live safely in seclusion as if within a moated, fortress wall. Like a feudal lord and protector, the head of the Brandybucks serves as Master of the Hall, the title passing from one generation to another, commanding great respect from the farmers.

Symbolism

Crossing the Brandywine River, the hobbits use a ferry which suggests the craft of Charon who carried the spirits of the dead across the River Styx to the Elysian Fields where virtuous people spend eternity, according to Greek mythology. Sam, uninitiated in river travel, comes closest to experiencing the intended symbolism. **Irony** then touches the mythological symbolism because, instead of transportation to the blessed isles, the hobbits head toward peril.

The three quest-bound hobbits splashing in the bath-water symbolically undergo the rite of baptism, which purifies an individual so that he may emerge from the sacrament a different person.

Fatty (Fredegar) Bolger represents the typical hobbit with no desire to leave the Shire. His horror of the Old Forest not only imparts a hobbit's natural fear of the eerie but also kindles anticipation of what will happen to the travelers. Fatty deserves merit, however, for promising to be the rear guard at Crickethollow and to inform Gandalf of what is happening.

Literary Style

Two poems break into the dialogue-filled narrative in which the hobbits confess their knowledge of Frodo's real aim to leave the Shire and offer to serve him. The bath song contrasts with the seriousness of the quest, revealing the child-like, playful behavior of the little creatures who love their comforts. The bath song, with its monotonous rhythm and simple rhyme scheme of a-a, b-b, etc., apostrophizes "Water Hot" as "a noble thing,"

The author skillfully chooses Merry and Pippin, the most child-like of the group, to sing a song patterned after the one Bilbo used long ago when he embarked on his adventures with the dwarves. The same rhythm and **rhyme** scheme as in the bath song deal with significant matter - visiting the Elves in Rivendell and encountering their foes. The light verse appropriately reveals the hobbits' ignorance about their future.

Characterization

The roles the characters will play firms up here. Childlike joy belongs to Pippin as in the case of great splashing in the bath. Both Pippin and Merry, the latter associated with practical yet pleasant aspects, pledge loyalty to Frodo in his plans to fight the "Enemy," preparing the reader for later allegiances they will readily make, Pippin testifies to Sam's loyalty. Sam emerges as chief investigator in the hobbits' conspiracy to unearth Frodo's plans. The credit for persuading Frodo not to go alone rests with Sam. His supportive role is strengthening. Frodo's leadership role appears definite as the hobbits call him Captain. Ever human, Frodo experiences relief at having companionship on the journey he was vowing to make alone.

CHAPTER 6, BOOK I: THE OLD FOREST

SUPERNATURAL ADVERSARIES

Personalized forces in nature thwart the hobbits and intriguingly portray one more aspect of malice Tolkien finds in the world. Paths which the hobbits want to take veer off in other directions, leading them unwillingly into the heart of the forest. The air itself becomes inimicable in the burning hot sun. Flies, reminiscent of the insect plagues which attack the Egyptians in the time of Moses, torment the hobbits. Uncontrollable sleep overtakes the travelers, recalling the Lotus Eaters who lulled Odysseus' men into a life of laziness and pleasure in *The Odyssey*. The sinister Barrow-Down with evil wights from a witch kingdom threaten the hobbits.

Trees offer unsurpassed menace in this chapter. Tolkien animates his trees with "reaching arms with many long-fingered hands." Frodo claims, "the beastly tree threw me in!'" And Merry reports that his tree will squeeze him in two if the fire is not extinguished. This introduces a new type of character into the fantasy. Old Man Willow, a menacing, arboraceous creature, seems to have stepped out of Walt Disney's first color cartoon, *Flowers and Trees* (1932) where natural objects seem to become human.

Even the hedge assumes human traits. The trees have long ago attacked the hedge by planting themselves in the middle of it. This brings to mind Robert Frost's line, "Something there is that doesn't like a wall" in his poem, "Mending Wall." Enmity exists between the trees and the hobbits who have cut away parts of the forest and made great bonfires. Superstition says that unfriendly trees attack people. This suggests the recently developed theory that plants have a unique, almost human sensitivity, expressing warnings of impending danger and experiencing distress.

The Old Forest strongly resembles the rough, savage growth of trees which the poet first encounters in his journey to the Inferno in *The Divine Comedy* by Dante Alighieri. The hobbits are, in fact, setting out for their own Inferno.

Deus ex Machina

Tolkien frequently resorts to a **deus ex machina** to rescue his hobbits like the appearance of the Elves in Chapter 3. This device - suddenly introducing a character or a happening to resolve a situation-often stands out as a literary flaw. With this author much improbability and artificiality diminishes since a character or event to resolve a problem seems unusually acceptable here because the reader of this fantasy is prepared to believe that anything can happen. Tom Bombadil, bearded and rosy-cheeked, answers Frodo's cry for help. Dressed in a tall-crowned hat, blue coat and yellow boots, he commands the willows to release their prisoners. The reader senses immediately that Tom is a perplexing and unique character who will unfold more fully in the next chapter.

This magical house gives Frodo a sense of timelessness, transporting him beyond hunger and weariness to wonder. Since Tolkien regards time as the enemy in man's fight against evil, he aptly clothes the goodness of the Bombadil house in timelessness.

Verity Techniques

Tolkien proves himself a master in handling magic materials by inserting sufficient realistic details to make the reader feel at home in the author's subcreation. Familiar food like bread and butter and cream and honey grace the table. The hobbits derive comfort from soft green slippers, squashy pillows and mattresses covered with white wool blankets. Touches like earthenware basins and brown ewers for bathing dispose the reader to believe the fantasy.

Symbolism

Tolkien's effective use of symbolism follows tradition. Tom and Goldberry represent the natural world. Tom possesses a unique moral neutrality beyond the confines of either heroism or villainy. The lilies which he brings his lady suggest purity and innocence. The flowering bean plants recall the belief that the scent makes people light-headed and silly. Green symbolizes hope, life and nature whereas yellow represents love, constancy and wisdom. These predominant colors are significant in Christianity. Goldberry's washing in the showers and her autumn housecleaning symbolize the purifying qualities of water. Candles illuminate the scene as if it were a religious ceremony.

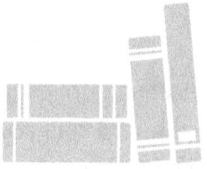

THE FELLOWSHIP OF THE RING

TEXTUAL ANALYSIS

PART 2

CHAPTER 7, BOOK I: IN THE HOUSE OF TOM BOMBADIL

Escape from the terrors of the Old Forest to Tom Bombadil's house follows Tolkien's pattern of shifting from horrors to havens.

Characterization

The hobbits' two benefactors are anomalies. Goldberry, daughter of the River, clad in green and silver, resembles the Earth Mother. She embodies the outgoing, uninhibited elements of Jean Jacques Rousseau's natural child in Emile. As Goldberry does her washing in rainwater, she resembles Nausicaa washing her linen at the river mouth in *The Odyssey*.

To Frodo's question of who is Tom Bombadil, Goldberry replies, "'He is.'" Tom himself says he is "'the Eldest,'" here before the creation of raindrops and acorns. He incorporates the Christian concept of stewardship, owning no growing things but being master of them all. Tom serves as an agent of an unnamed providence or fate in rescuing the hobbits. To the hobbits' amazement he remains impervious to the ring. In fact, he makes it disappear.

Structure

Chapter 7 resembles a musical comedy. Gay and lyrical, the substance forwards the story with dialogue, songs, and even dances. Swinging lamps and many yellow candles illuminate the colorful setting. Goldberry sits as if enthroned with white water lilies at her feet Tom's songs fill the house. The hobbits, drinking a clear liquid, sing merrily in preference to talking.

Dream sequences appear as if on revolving stage sets.

Literary Style

Poetry figures prominently in this chapter. Tom Bombadil's songs fit the gangling creature who resembles the Scarecrow in *The Wizard of Oz* by Frank Baum. Tom uses rhymed verse punctuated with nonsense language. Nonsense language may convey little if any meaning literally but linguistic studies indicate that sounds, whether a structured part of language or not, express emotions. Tom's phrases possess an appropriate exuberance. They resemble some songs in Shakespeare's works like the following lines from *As You like It:* "It was a lover with his lass, /With a hey, and a ho, and a hey nonino,…"

Dreams

A recurring favorite of Tolkien, the use of dreams, here serves a purpose which will become clear only later. Frodo's dream of the lone figure of a man being borne away from a pinnacle by an eagle suggests Gandalf with his white hair and his staff. Pippin's dream relives the experience of being captured by the willow tree. Merry's dream of drowning reconfirms the hobbits' fear of water. These dreams serve to keep alive the dreads which await the hobbits even with Goldberry's reassurance, "'Have peace...Heed no nightly noise.'" Artistically this keeps a balance between the ideal safety of the present and the actual horrors in store.

Metaphorical Language

Beauty largely characterizes the descriptions such as the one of Goldberry resembling a young elf-queen "clad in living flowers." Tom's whistling sounds like a starling. Near the house the red flowers on the beans began "to glow against the wet green leaves." Goldberry's rain-song sounds as sweet as rain on dry hills. Rain makes the "white chalky path turn into a little river of milk." "The young Sun shone like fire on the red metal of their new and greedy swords." This describes ancient wars.

CHAPTER 8, BOOK I: FOG ON THE BARROW DOWNS

Christian Aspects

Though nowhere does Tolkien refer to God or an orthodox church, Christian aspects emerge in Frodo's action of laying down his life for his friends. Rollo May, in Power and Innocence, describes Frodo's type of bravery. "...physical courage in whatever scene...seems to hinge on whether the individual can feel he is fighting for others as well as himself, assuming a bond with his fellows, which means he will come to their aid as they will to his." Even imprisoned, Frodo musters a song of help to Tom Bombadil. Tom resembles the Good Shepherd in leading the hobbits to a green, sunlit barrow. His renaming Merry's five ponies creates an Adam picture where the first man named the animals of the earth. He also conjures a vision of ancient warriors against evil.

Symbolism

The Barrow-wights represent evil, casting strange spells over the hobbits. Arthurian legends furnish one traditional source for spell-casting when Vivien imprisoned Merlin in a tree. Tolkien equates darkness with evil. As the barrow-wights gain control, darkness encompasses Frodo. The golden, bejeweled treasure which Tom discovers shows the author's tendency to relate materialism with evil.

Descriptive Language

Stones stand "like jagged teeth," resembling Stonehenge. Fog appears, like a roof. The brooch Tom selects for Goldberry from the treasure has blue stones "many-shaded like...wings of blue butterflies."

CHAPTER 9, BOOK I: AT THE SIGN OF THE PRANCING PONY

Structure

The novel, episodic in nature, focuses here on adventures at the Inn in Bree which continues through the following chapter and into Chapter 11. Elements of the traditional detective story appear. The suspicious gatekeeper who finally lets the hobbits in sets the stage for mystery as does a dark figure climbing unnoticed over the gate. Mistaken identity, a detective-story gimmick, emerges with Strider, one of the Rangers who later reveals his real name. Even a lost letter turns up, containing a valuable message from Gandalf. Barliman Butterbur, the innkeeper, who has forgotten to deliver the letter, appears a Dr. Watson type, talking more than he thinks, needing explanations spelled out for him.

Characterization

Mr. Butterbur exemplifies Tolkien's tendency to produce stock characters as background figures. He pampers his guests and high-handedly gives orders to his helpers, Nob and Bob. His merriment and hospitality with tasty food and conviviality in the common rooms reminds the reader of the innkeeper of the Tabard Inn in Chaucer's *Canterbury Tales*.

The strange looking weather-beaten man, Strider, bearing signs of travel on his heavy clothing, sets a serious, even ominous tone. He indicates an intimate knowledge of the mission of Frodo and the hobbits. He emerges as a father figure, protective, wise.

Humor

The innkeeper and his helpers fall in the comic category. Humor also encompasses the scene in which Frodo disappears, notwithstanding the dire portents of having revealed his ownership of the ring and its magic properties.

Frodo's rendering of Bilbo's nursery-rhyme song adds amusement. It parodies the familiar "Hey, Diddle, Diddle" Mother Goose verse with the characters of the Man in the Moon, personified spoons and forks, a cat and a dog and a tipsy osler.

Tone

An unusual combination of conviviality and impending doom adds tension to this chapter. The complacency of the Shire hobbits gives away to uneasiness and fear as they become aware of people who are fleeing danger in the South. Hints about the rights of people to live surface. The mysterious breed of wanderers called Rangers, with their ability to understand the language of birds and bees, contributes to the eerie atmosphere. Gaiety and fellowship of the evening at the Sign of the Prancing Pony thinly veneers imminent danger to the traveling hobbits.

CHAPTER 10, BOOK I: STRIDER

Function

Strider's talk with Frodo reveals his function in the plot-to enlarge the fellowship of the four hobbits and to provide a traditional hero-type of leader. He functions as a protector of the good, cautioning Frodo about Bill Ferny. His familiarity with the poem in Gandalf's letters confirms Strider's identity as Aragorn, son of Arathorn. He explains the baffling lines, "Renewed shall be the blade that was broken."

Outside, alone in the dark, Merry succumbs to the Black Breath, pinpointing the hobbit's childishness and naivite. A similar type of evil overpowered the Red Cross Knight in his encounter with the monster in the cave in *The Faerie Queen*.

The artistry and information in Gandalf's misplaced letter quicken the reader's interest. His rune marks the message in several places. This word from Gandalf encourages the hobbits; however, with Tolkien, the good usually appears weaker than the bad.

Point Of View

The point of view remains with Frodo. Tolkien is delving more deeply into Frodo's mind for the purpose of showing character development in this central figure in the trilogy. The external view of the little hobbit's manfully trying to show courage to Strider belies the inner quakings of this elected creature.

Allusions

Gandalf's poem baffles the hobbits with two different classifications of allusions, general and specific. A literary puzzle, its general references give clues to the entire story of the trilogy. **Allusions** to objects in nature, "deep roots," "frost," "ashes," and "light from the shadows," couch the main story line obscurely in traditional **imagery**. More specific references,

"All that is gold does not glitter, Not all those who wander are lost" bear directly on Aragorn as do the two last lines about the broken sword and the crownless king. The broken sword of the mythic hero draws on Wagner's Siegfried in which the title hero forges his own sword.

An astronomical **allusion** occurs when Frodo sees the Sickle, the hobbit name for the Great Bear, shining brightly over Bree. Ancient European legends indicate widespread fear of wild bears so the Great Bear might forecast fear for the hobbits.

Theme Of Evil

Tolkien enlarges on his overall **theme** of evil which is pervading the world. Strider adds a new dimension in locating the genesis of evil in Mordor, the land of Sauron, the arch enemy. Evil personified, the Black Riders, from whom emanate the Black Breath which overcomes Merry, attack in darkness and loneliness. These deadly wraiths triumph through fear techniques. Strider explains that their power is in terror.

CHAPTER 11, BOOK I: A KNIFE IN THE DARK

Chapter 11 really climaxes the adventures begun in Chapter 9 at the Prancing Pony with much more action and building tension.

Quest Of The Hobbits

The departure from Bree attracts much attention as the hobbits with Strider parade through the main street en route to a noble mission. Traditional heroes going on quests as recorded in literature leave with fanfare on sleek steeds with high purposes in mind. This group inverts the quest concept, trudging on foot, two by two, with Sam in the rear leading a pathetic pony. (All of Merry's ponies have fled Bree.) While ultimately their quest will become heroic in purpose, the present destination is Rivendell, the Elven refuge.

Tolkien draws on the **epic**, *Le Chanson de Roland,* in the scene where Fatty Bolger, on guard at Frodo's new home, Crickhollow, calls for rescue from three black figures from Mordor. Roland's horn-alarm system to summon Charlemagne to his aid failed because of too long a delay but the Horn-call of Bucklands alerts the community to danger in good time, being blown for the first time since the white wolves' attack of the Fell Winter.

Humor

Tolkien's injection of gentle humor distorts the seriousness accompanying literary quests. In the loss of the horses. "Mr. Butterbur knew his money was "gone for good, or for bad." Bill Ferny parodies the stock type villain. Sam, attacking Bill, hits him in the nose with an apple. "Waste of a good apple," Sam calls it.

Types Of Evil

In the Midgewater Marshes the group encounters flies and midgies which bite them relentlessly, these insects being evil animated. Bill Ferny exemplifies evil personified as do Frodo's assailants. He sees five of the black-robed enemy with gray garb beneath, merciless and haggard. The chief attacker resembles the gaunt knight in "La Belle Dame Sans Merci" by John Keats, as he assaults Frodo with knife and sword. Meanwhile, the power of the ring, evil objectified, has clutched Frodo. As he puts the ring on his finger, he sees evil personified clearly, indicating Tolkien's belief that evil frequently conquers and corrupts good, causing disaster.

Legend

Tolkien masters the making of legends with an ancient lay of his own, The Fall of Gil-galad, which Sam sings, having learned it from Bilbo. The name of Gil-galad, last of the great Elf kings, means Starlight. Strider chants the love story of Beren, a mortal hero, and Tinuviel which means Nightingale in the ancient language.

Both songs resemble ballads, telling sentimentalized stories in identical iambic rhythm with simple wording though without a repeated **refrain**. The subject matter of both stories focuses on high-born creatures as is frequently the case in ballads. The tale of Tinuviel and Beren relates a tragic love story, the most popular topic in ballads. Both songs have been perpetuated by oral tradition as is customary with ballads.

CHAPTER 12, BOOK I: FLIGHT TO THE FORD

Characterization

As peril closes in on the sojourners, characters develop and grow. Sam's ever-increasing devotion to his master manifests itself in his tears over Frodo's wound. His unmerited suspicion of Strider causes the little hobbit to draw his sword to protect Frodo. He will, in fact, guard his master at the sacrifice of self. He angrily defends his master's weakness as Glorfindel insists that the company move on to the Ford.

Several acts delineate Pippin's childishness. He shows candid surprise at Strider's knowledge of his people. He impulsively identifies as live and dangerous trolls the three troll shapes which Gandalf had long ago turned into stone when the trolls were quarreling over the right way to cook thirteen dwarves and one hobbit (Bilbo). He puts up a front to hide his fears.

In his treatment of the hobbits, Strider emerges as a protective, paternal figure with considerable grace, understanding, and wisdom. The first inkling that he will become a larger-than-life figure appears in his exceptional ability to heal. He sings a slow song in a foreign tongue and bathes Frodo's wound with a fragrant herb solution made from the little known plant called Athelas. Strider, acting as scout, cases the territory to avoid the enemy. He keeps vigil through the night while the others sleep.

Glorfindel the Elf also presents a fine figure with humanity and wisdom. His traveling experience has informed him of the location of the enemy. He warily plans the company's advance to the Ford, giving Frodo his own steed to ride.

Supernatural Elements

The evil type of supernatural elements outnumber the good as always in this novel though both effect changes. Athelas, the rare herb, possesses magical properties. Glorfindel's drink for the hungry band enables them to gain vigor. Strider finds a beryl, an Elf stone, which he hopefully takes as a sign that they may be able to pass the bridge safely.

But the bad seems to overpower the good. The enemy's weapon wounds Frodo not only physically but spiritually. Giant trolls, legacies from Scandinavian folk lore who live in caves, portend danger. Adversaries, trying to wrest the ring from Frodo, wraith-like creatures, have overpowering wills.

Symbolism

Tolkien employs symbolism to convey the meaning of the supernatural. The pale king who attacks Frodo represents death traditionally and, in this case, more particularly spiritual death. Black conventionally symbolizes evil and the shimmering white of Glorfindel's clothing and horse, the good. Cold also represents evil. Frodo under the spell of his wound experiences chill. A mist frequently obscures his vision, indicating the barrier of evil which is preventing him from seeing the truth.

The purifying quality of water in traditional symbolism protects Frodo as the river rises high to wash away evil. Biblical symbolism emerges in the concluding scene when the river at flood stage destroys the enemy. The dramatic conclusion to Book I shows that the angry white foam, resembling "white riders upon white horses with frothing manes," overwhelms Frodo's attackers. Implying an overall purpose in events in nature, this scene draws on the escape of Moses and the children of Israel from the pursuing Egyptians who perished as the divided Red Sea closed up and drowned the advancing hord.

CHAPTER I, BOOK II: MANY MEETINGS

Characterization

Variety hits the keynote for characters here. The Ranger, Strider, hearty, weather-beaten man in the mold of the American cowboy, gains dimension. Gandalf reveals that Strider is Aragorn, the Dunadan, son of Arathorn of the race of the Kings from across the Sea, a Man of the West, Numenorean. The word Numenorean may well be derived from the Roman mythological term numen, meaning a presiding spirit or divinity. Dunadan seems to be rooted in the ancient term dun, a fortified enclosure in which Irish kings of old and their nobles dwelt. His greatness as an awe-inspiring person stretches out toward Frodo to protect the little hobbit.

Sam's role as faithful servant keeps him at his wounded master's bedside, urging Frodo to get his rest. Change is making its mark on the ringbearer although Elrond has successfully removed the splinter of the evil sword so that Frodo does not fall completely under the sway of Sauron's forces. Gandalf talks of Frodo's strength and resistance. Frodo's courage, coupled with fate or fortune, has enabled him to escape the Dark Lord. Frodo exemplifies the durability for which hobbits are noted.

Supernatural Elements

Tolkien populates this chapter with multiple supernatural elements ranging from the peculiar power of the Black Rider to wound Frodo both physically and spiritually to the traditional werewolves, man-devouring humans changed into beasts. Like werewolves, the wargs, also evil wolves, serve Sauron, as do orcs and trolls. The name orc suggests Orcus, the synonym for Pluto or Dis, god of the Underworld. In Greek the word means oath. Probably the god of the underworld punished perjuries. Later European tradition reveals him as a maneating forest sprite, hairy and black, who probably became the ogre of fairy tales. Similarly the name of the Morgul-Lord harks back to the root word for death. These personifications of evil feature coldness and nothingness as their principal characteristics much in the manner of Joseph Conrad's concept of evil in *The Heart of Darkness*.

The ageless Elrond, the Elven Lord of Rivendell, possesses unique powers as seen in his ability to command the flood which has overpowered the Dark Riders at the Ford. Glorfindel occupies a place second to Elrond among the Elves and has likewise proved himself a protector of the hobbits. Gandalf stacks up well in this category, a bushy-browed figure full of wisdom like Merlin in the King Arthur legend. Another greatly needed ally, Grimbeorn, son of Beorn, guards the High Pass and the Ford of Carrock against orcs.

Between the peaks of good and bad stands the sturdy dwarf, Gimli, of the breed of underground supernatural kings. Gimli, resembling "Court Dwarves" of Velasquez, suggests Una's dwarf companion in *The Faerie Queen*. His wealth of information about his fellow creatures edifies the travelers.

Literary Style

Dialogue provides information to fill in the gaps about Frodo's wound. Bilbo's long song about the mariner king, Earendil, punctuates the many conversational passages. The song to Elbereth sung in the Elven tongue, evidences Tolkien's interest in creating a language with characteristics of the ancient speech familiar to him as a scholar.

Lyrical descriptions appear in Tolkien's chapters centered on good. In this connection, note his descriptions of Elrond and Aragorn.

CHAPTER 2, BOOK II: THE COUNCIL OF ELROND

This chapter, the longest in *The Fellowship of the Ring*, marks a highpoint as members of the Middle Earth community tell their stories, thereby completing the history of the ring. All of the preceding material in the novel melts into a unified whole at this meeting which increases the little band of sojourners to the Fellowship of the Nine.

Medieval Features

Tolkien's knowledge of medieval literature manifests itself in a number of ways. The Council of Elrond resembles the gathering of the knights in *Beowulf* in the great mead-hall. Boromir's silver-tipped horn harks back to Norse mythology in which Heimdall, watchman of the gods, had Giallarhorn to sound alarm in case of attack. The broken sword motif stems from medieval literature which abounds in magic swords as in the case of the Arthurian legends and Wagner's *Nibelungenlied*. The monster Gollum derives from a bevy of creatures, half-animal, half-human, like the centaur. His escape from captivity by the Elves forebodes no good.

Radagast the Brown as a wizard joins Gandalf in this figure familiar in the King Arthur legend in the form of Merlin.

Gandalf's imprisonment, strictly medieval, on a pinnacle of Orthanc, recalls the dank, cold cell of Lord Byron's poem, "The Prisoner of Chillon." Saruman, albeit lying, cites the Round Table goals of Knowledge, Rule and Order. The idea of the magic horses like Shadowflax which carries Gandalf to safety after his rescue stems from medieval lore. Classic origins in Greek mythology offer the eagle as the king of the birds, dear to Zeus and, therefore, safe from lightning bolts. Such was Gandalf's rescuer, Gwaihir the Windlord, swiftest of all eagles.

Dovetailing

Information revealed in long stories told at the Council has a major impact on the plot, all dovetailing into a unified plot centering on the ring. Aragorn's narrative about the capture of the slimy Gollum leads into Legolas' dutiful confession that Gollum has, in fact, escaped. Gandalf contributes details to the perfidy of the wizard, Saruman. Isildur's scroll describes the Great Ring with its Elven inscription. The reader now grasps the power of the ring to enmesh all different kinds of creatures in its sway.

Themes

Evil, the overall **theme** of this novel, has many by-products. Gandalf warns of the decline of the great Men of the West with courage to combat evil. The end of this breed will allow depravity to triumph much in the fashion that decadence of the Roman Empire aided the victory of the barbarians. Sauron, according to Elrond's story, exemplifies one concept-that nothing is evil in the beginning. A classic example is the band of fallen angels, outcasts from Paradise. Aragorn speaks of the simple folk, free from care and worry, although evil lurks close by, unrecognized. Their goodness resembles that of Billy Budd in Herman Melville's novel, *Billy Budd, Foretopman*, in which the Christ-like innocence of the title character becomes a target for evil forces.

The novel's pervasive wickedness, like Proteus in Greek mythology, assumes many forms: the ring itself, the Shadow, the black horsemen, the slimy creature named Gollum, the Necromancer in Dol Guldur who turns out to be Sauron in disguise. But with evil alive in the world the underlying implication of an overall purpose in the universe emerges in Gandalf's observation that the escaped Gollum may play a part in all of this as yet unseen.

Symbolism

Although Tolkien decries any resemblance to contemporary affairs, the ring inevitably begins to resemble World War II events with a Shadow lengthening on an area, a frightened people ready to yield. Autumn suggests the waning of the lush, natural growth, a prelude to winter with the coldness of evil pervading the word.

Interesting symbolic use of colors rises when Gandalf the Grey calls his colleague Saruman the White. Gandalf's grey indicates that the wizard is transforming into a greater, purer figure whereas Saruman insists on being Saruman of Many Colors, defiling the purity of white as he sinks into evil. In the landscape of Orthanc dark smoke clings to all his works.

The most significant symbolism lies in the White Tree, a sapling from the White Tree which grew in the King's Court in Numenor, representing the diminished line of great men of Numenor, the once powerful kingdom of the Dunedain. The dried tree stands, awaiting replacement, tied in with Bilbo's remark about having a happy ending to his book. The remark, premature at the time, suggests the eucatastrophe which Tolkien terms as the proper ending, a brief vision of an underlying truth or reality.

THE FELLOWSHIP OF THE RING

TEXTUAL ANALYSIS

PART 3

CHAPTER 3, BOOK II: THE RING GOES SOUTH

Chapter 3 initiates a period of waiting like a prestorm calm as scouts search for traces of the enemy. Then an immediate shift to action occurs, unlike the novel's usual pattern, as the fellowship begins its quest. The band struggles against the forces of nature.

Fellowship Of Free People

"'The Company of the Ring shall be Nine; and the Nine Walkers shall be set against the Nine Riders that are evil ...'" Gandalf, Legolas of the Elves, Gimli of the Dwarves, Aragorn and Boromir of men and the four hobbits, Frodo, Sam, Merry and Pippin compose the Company of the Ring.

Their weapons to fight evil show medieval influence. Aragorn carries the Sword of Elendil which has been reforged and renamed Anduril. Frodo takes Bilbo's sword, Sting, and his dwarf armor. Legolas carries a long white knife, a bow and a quiver of arrows, much in the manner of the Huntsman in Chaucer's *Canterbury Tales*. Boromir has a shield, a long sword, and his war-horn. Gandalf with the Elven sword Glamdring at his side carries his staff like that of the archetype of high priests Aaron. Also, the palmer in *The Faerie Queen* carries a staff. But for all the weapons their hopes lie not in combat but in secrecy.

"Their purpose was to hold this course west of the Mountains ..." This uses the idea from Tennyson's poem, "Ulysses," as the aged hero sets out on his last quest. "For my purpose holds to sail beyond the sunset ..."

An overall purpose of the mission exists - the ultimate destruction of the ring (Elrond gives this charge to Frodo) - but immediate aims include wiping out the enemy, the Ringwraiths, who are seemingly indestructible because with Tolkien the power of evil has an all-threatening strength.

Tolkien's Literary Style

The sound of language fell meaningfully on Tolkien's ears. Scouts cover such geographical regions as Hoarwell and Ettenmoors, the Greyflood, Mirkwood, Gladden Fields and Wilderland, areas out of the author's imagination with lyrical sounds. Equally poetic is miruvor, Gandalf's magic portion from Rivendell, and the Dimrill Stair, a high pass. A description of the Sword of Elendil makes the fine blade visible in the mind's eye with its ornamentation. Bilbo's dwarf-mail is "as supple almost as linen, cold as ice, and harder than steel." Because Frodo wears this under his breeches, tunic and jacket, it symbolizes an inner, invisible strength in the little hobbit.

Tolkien describes the winter day of departure with romantic tendencies to beautify aspects of nature. Bilbo's song about remembering things he has seen focuses on idealized aspects of nature like "meadow-flowers" and "silver sun." The mountain, Caradhras, personified, possesses an ill will and malice, threatening the Company with a snow storm and, at the chapter's end, defeating them.

The territory of Hollin with its red-berried holly trees swarms with crow-like birds who spy on the travelers. The author calls them crebains. This sound connotes ugliness whereas the choice of words, for the most part here, indicates traditional lyricism.

CHAPTER 4, BOOK II: A JOURNEY IN THE DARK

Characterization

Frodo with his responsibility as ringbearer develops gradually. Though he longs to abandon his role, he cannot condone the shame and defeat this would bring. The grim wound from the orcs has left Frodo with acute senses and sharper awareness. He can even see better in the dark than his fellow travelers. A deep anxiety over the presence of evil is clutching him.

Growing more faithful, Sam suffers a terrible wrench at the loss of his beloved pony, who bolts at the presence of evil and flees to the outside world of wolves and snakes. Sam's nobility and unselfishness foreshadows an even greater sacrifice he will make for the ringbearer.

Gandalf exhibits leadership ability as he imperiously takes the frightened band through the Doors of Durin, Lord of Moria, in Khazad-Dum, straight to the tomb of Balin, son of Fundin. Gandalf always make the final decisions about where to travel, holding his staff aloft at times, emanating mystical qualities.

Pippin presents a contrasting quality-childishness. Different from the maturing devotion of Sam, Pippin's selfishness manifests itself as he brightens visibly at a remote chance to turn back from dangers. He says flatly he does not wish to enter Moria. Ever childlike, Pippin finds himself curiously attracted to a deep well. Impulse compels him to drop a stone into the well, disturbing the unidentified evil creature below.

Gimli grows in stature as he displays historical knowledge about the dwarves, especially in his chant-type song about Durin who built up the great realm and city of Dwarrowdelf (or Khazad-Dum) in an age of light and splendor. Traveling there now, the Fellowship finds darkness "In Moria, in Khazad-Dum," which brings to mind Samuel Taylor Coleridge's poem about building the pleasure palace in "Kubla Khan." Gimli reveals deep devotion to his people at Balin's tomb.

Verity Techniques

The supernatural world inhabited by orcs and wargs, like Death at Hell-Gate in Milton's Paradise Lost, contains the magical Dwarf-Doors which open only at the proper command from Gandalf. Sting and Glamdring, Frodo's and Gandalf's swords, possess the magical quality of giving off a cold light in the presence of orcs. The lode of mithril, the true silver which makes for the wealth of Moria, does not come of the real world.

The author brings credibility to the supernatural by his own illustrations of the magic doors, complete with Elven inscriptions. Gandalf's power makes visible the doors which shine only in the moonlight. Balin's tomb, an oblong slab capped with a white stone as real as any tomb, bears an Elven inscription which the author depicts in its original characters. Gandalf can translate the words. The landscape with its lake and cliffs and giant holly trees present a familiar world. The huge, empty halls resemble a worldly castle with many stairs and passages. Gimli's song, telling the legend of Durin, who is expected to rise from the dead someday, gives a historical aura to the supernatural. Gimli, the living dwarf, provides a bridge to this older world removed from the current creation of Tolkien's imagination.

CHAPTER 5, BOOK II: THE BRIDGE AT KHAZAD-DUM

This dramatic chapter, action-packed in part, brings the Fellowship into a major conflict with the orcs, evil personified in more distinctive descriptions than have appeared before. Whereas Chapter 4 suggests the mysterious presence of the enemy, Chapter 5 comes out in forthright combat.

Historical Allusions

Tolkien neatly inserts many historical **allusions** which give substance to his fantasy world. The discovery of the Book of Mazarbul chronicles Balin's expedition to Khazad-Dum which has ended in death for the dwarves at the hands of the orcs. Gimli rightly keeps the ancient record, another medieval crutch which Tolkien uses in the manner of Chretien de Troyes. When trapped, Oin, Ori, Frar, Loni, Nali and, of course, Balin met their deaths at the hands of orcs.

Supernatural Elements

This chapter contains a preponderance of supernatural elements in action. The caverns of Moria begin to echo with a deep "doom doom" of the enemies' drums, suggesting eerie voodoo practices. Orcs, of course, appear to attack as well as the Black Uruks of Mordor, large and evil, and a couple of cave trolls. We here see an orc chieftain through Tolkien's words as "almost man high." He had "a great, flat, toeless foot." Aragorn's sword Anduril splits the chieftain's head. Gandalf uses a shutting spell on the door. A Balrog appears with great griffin-like wings. Gandalf's sword Glamdring glitters white in the weapons exchange with the Balrog whose sword flies into fragments. The Balrog is also known as Durin's Bane because of his murder of Durin IV. In the conflict Gandalf's staff breaks in two, representing symbolically the end of his service as leader. White flames spring up as it falls and the bridge cracks, causing the Balrog to drop into emptiness. The powerful forces of evil varyingly portrayed here triumph as the Balrog succeeds in capturing Gandalf with his whip and pulling the wizard into the abyss.

Action Scenes

In this chapter Tolkien reveals himself a master at depicting actual combat, using multiple details, meticulously chosen as when he describes landscapes, fantastic abodes, jewels, and raiments. He manages to create high suspense even though the usual length of his sentences remains unchanged. The enemy comes singly as in the case of the orc chieftain, the Balrog and the orc which Frodo stabs with Sting - a monster with "skin of greenish scales." They also come en masse, a group beyond counting. The highpoint of the action occurs in Gandalf's fight with the Balrog, face to face on the narrow bridge which has no railing. After both fall into the abyss, the company stands with horror, "staring into the pit."

CHAPTER 6, BOOK II: LOTHLORIEN

History of Dwarves and Elves

The new geographical area which the Fellowship now invades contains lore of the dwarves, another testament to Tolkien's ability to create purely imaginative history. The Mountains of Moria are significantly three in number. Legend supplies the reason why the Elven folk in Lorien dwell in trees-Nimrodel was said to have built a tree house. These Elves, called the Galadrim, the Tree People, offer hospitality of an un-hobbit variety for hobbits love to be underground. In Cerin Amroth, the ancient realm of the friendly Elven folk, the Fellowship gains understanding of their new hosts.

Bits from the Other World

Tolkien offers largely a pleasant brand of supernatural elements here in relieving contrast to evil. Extraordinarily tall trees, known as mellryn or mallorn, bearing golden flowers, bloom in ever-green grass at the mound of Amroth. Aragorn produces a healing herb in treating Sam's sand Frodo's wounds. This incident reveals to the Fellowship Frodo's underneath corselet of mithril which has the magical property to protect its wearer like the green girdle which Sir Gawain wore for immunity against harm in Sir Gawain and the Green Knight. An unearthly element of timelessness grasps Frodo. The mysterious patter of feet and two strange gleams of light dog Frodo's steps. The host Elves themselves, Haldir, Rumil and Orophin, guarding the borders of

Lorien, display common sense in insuring their own safety and appear to be very human creatures although supernatural.

Autobiographical Elements

Several bits related to Tolkien himself crop up here. Frodo's wounds may be compared to the wounds the author suffered in World War I. His love of ancient lore and his medieval scholarship are evidenced in the secondary Elven world he creates with the stock supernatural creatures which abound in the literature of that period. As a lover of language, he possesses remarkable ability to create words and to use obsolete or seldom-heard terms. Examples abound - "sward" for grasscovered soil, "westering" for moving west, "sickle" for the crescent moon, "gaffer" for an old man, "flet" or "talan" for tree houses. Several Elven words occur untranslated though remarkably understandable like "Yrch," "Daro," and "Arwen vanimelda, namarie!" The last terms express Aragorn's longing for his Elven lady love.

CHAPTER 7, BOOK II: THE MIRROR OF GALADRIEL

The Fellowship's stay at Caras Galadon, the court of Lord Celeborn and Galadriel, the Lady of Lorien, provides a refreshing respite amid the many large telain (plural of talan) in a grove of mellryn trees. The purpose of this chapter is to increase Frodo's knowledge of the ring and the troubled times in the Shire.

Characterization

The introduction of a new king and queen provides character contrasts. Oddly enough, Galadriel makes a much more impressive figure than her husband. The Lady of Lorien's hair is deep gold while Celeborn's is silver white. Galadriel resembles Goldberry in her ethereal loveliness and her protective attitude towards the Fellowship. Her words are Christ-like, offering them peace throughout the night. At other times Galadriel appears to be a temptress, testing the travelers as to their real desire to continue on the quest. Yet in her own moment of temptation when the possession of the ring lies within her grasp, she becomes incredibly tall, beautiful and worshipful. As she resists evil, she shrinks again into an Elven woman. She exemplifies the Christian **theme** of loving one's enemies as she shows affection and understanding of the dwarf, Gimli. (The **theme** repeats in the relationship between Legolas and Gimli who now travel about together among the Galadrim.)

Frodo shows growth in character and perception in noting Galadriel's desire for the ring. This sensitivity to the magic of the place appears heightened. His grief at the passing of Gandalf is so genuine that he is able to compose a poetic lamentation eulogizing the wizard. Galadriel informs this reader that Frodo will grow more in stature as his testing has only begun.

Mirror of Galadriel

The Mirror of Galadriel emerges as a special anomaly in this highly imaginative kingdom which imbues the readers with credulity. Caras Galadon, in the first place, resembles a medieval fortress, its wall and heavy gates enclosing a City of Trees with a meeting house typical of castles. The company sleeps on couches provided by the Elves in a sylvan setting which recalls the gathering of the fairies in Shakespeare's play, *A Midsummer Night's Dream.*

Such a spot as this gives credence to the mystical powers of the Mirror of Galadriel which reveals many visions. The dark waters in the basin show Sam a glimpse of future adventures which he cannot understand—Frodo sleeping under a great cliff, himself climbing a winding stair. A present view of the Shire discloses a factory built on the site of the Old Mill. His grandfather has been ousted from Bagshot Row. Frodo finds difficulty, too, in understanding the visions he sees—Gandalf clothed in white, not grey, Bilbo's restlessly walking in his room, the sea in a storm, a blazing sun and a seven-towered fortress, the smoke of battle, a banner with a white tree as its emblem, and a small ship vanishing on the horizon. Frodo's incomprehensible montage of visions reaches a **climax** with the Eye "yellow as a cat's" and "rimmed with fire." In the center, there is nothingness, the same description of evil used by Conrad in *Heart of Darkness*. Frodo feels drawn to evil, knowing that the Eye is looking for him, the ringbearer.

Magic mirrors play a significant role in medieval literature. "The Squire's Tale" in Chaucer's *Canterbury Tales* features a magic mirror, a gift from Prester John, which allows one to see any adversity or enemy in its glass. Britomart of Spenser's *The Faerie Queen* envisions the image of her lover in a magic mirror. The fairy tale of "Snow White and the Seven Dwarfs," which furnished Walt Disney with material for the first full-length animated cartoon, has a magic mirror. This tells a wicked queen that she is not "the fairest one of all."

CHAPTER 8, BOOK II: FAREWELL TO LORIEN

Despite what appears to be movement this chapter contains a static quality, almost an elongation of the Company's stay at Caras Galadon under the protection of Celeborn and Galadriel.

Characterization

Two important character developments take precedence in interest over the uneventful journey of ten miles by boat away from Lorien. As Boromir discusses his purpose to go to Minas Tirith, the chief city of Gondor, he makes a slip in speaking, implying that it is folly to throw the ring away. Hastily correcting this, he takes on a strange and new facial expression which Frodo notices.

Aragorn shoulders the burden of taking over for the lost Gandalf. His summons, as heir of Elendil, to triumph over Sauron causes an internal conflict as he sees his new responsibility of leadership for the Fellowship of the ring. Aragorn exemplifies Tolkien's belief in an individual's right to exercise free will. This belief Legolas emphasizes in his remark to Gimli.

Swan Motif

Galadriel and Celeborn appear for the farewell feast in a Swan-ship with the queen singing and playing the harp. Swans figure prominently in medieval literature. Unusually familiar is the swan boat which brings Lohengrin to Elsa's rescue in Wagner's opera, Lohengrin. The swan of Lohengrin, son of Parsifal, relates to the holy and mystical world. Tolkien indubitably wished to make this connection with the royal couple who, without being so named, symbolize many aspects of Christianity.

Dramatic Elements

In a constantly threatening atmosphere, Tolkien skillfully manages to highlight this chapter's two dramatic **episodes** - the boats at Sarn Gebir and the attack by orcs. The rapids on the Anduin River cannot be navigated; the little band traveling by night approaches Sarn Gebir unawares until Sam calls out a last-ditch warning. They can make small headway in the battle against the current which carries them nearer and nearer to the eastern bank. Suddenly black-feathered arrows whistle through the night. Frodo's hidden mithril mail saves him from another wound. They somehow get to the western shore, a haven of comparative safety, only to see a great creature, "blacker than the pits of night," in the sky. Legolas' sure arrow from his Lorien bow drops the enemy. The scene provides exciting action which mounts, arriving at a **climax**, and then falls off to a brief denouement.

Characterization

Amid the action a couple of incidents speak to character development. Aragorn beholds Argonath, the Pillars of Kings, two gigantic, awesome statues of the kings, Isildur and Anarion. The sight of these ancestral monuments inspires in Aragorn a sense of pride and destiny. He is no longer the weather-beaten Strider but a king returning to his own land from exile, a special light in his eyes. Aragorn is becoming more of a King Arthur figure, a legendary hero to lead his people.

Boromir's notable restlessness gives the reader pause for speculation, as does the queer gleam in his eye as he looks at Frodo. Sam takes the role of watchman, predicting later assignments of this nature. He watches out for Gollum to protect Frodo. He watches the waters as the boats approach the rapids, crying out warnings just in time.

Personification of Evil

Two different personifications of evil lurk dangerously near the sojourners-Gollum traveling down the stream on a log and the armed orcs ashore. Tolkien has refined his personifications which stem from such literary works as John Bunyan's *Pilgrim's Progress*. Bunyan names his sins outright - Sloth, Hypocrisy, and the like. Virtues like Piety and Charity receive the names of the qualities they represent. Areas like the Slough of Despond also lack subtlety in Bunyan's allegory. Tolkien's evil personages from his own secondary world operate in bleak, withered Brown Lands in the cold of winter where often fog shrouds the path. The author's symbolism pervades his work.

Language

A lover of quaint and obsolete words, Tolkien sprays the pages generously with terms like "wold," "fen and tussock," "Eyot," and "wind-writhen." How much more intriguing are words like this than treeless plain, bogs and clumps of grass, and a rocky island! The "rind of a new moon" refreshingly describes the usual slim crescent in the sky.

CHAPTER 10, BOOK II: THE BREAKING OF THE FELLOWSHIP

The final chapter in *The Fellowship of the Ring* sows the seeds for the sequel, The Two Towers. At last the ringbearer with his faithful Sam leaves the Company to undertake his dangerous mission.

Dramatic Highpoints

The scene in which Boromir confronts Frodo demanding that the ring be saved presents a David and Goliath picture with Boromir the Man towering over the innocent, righteous little hobbit. The Eye also attacks the ringbearer with its fierce, eager will. Frodo crouches and covers his head with his hood. Vivid indeed is Frodo's inner conflict with the power of evil and the power of good struggling equally inside. From the struggle of his own voice against the Eye Frodo emerges as himself, a creature of free will, able to act independently.

Sam's desperate attempt to halt the fleeing and invisible master almost ends in disaster as Sam's efforts to reach what appears to be a rower-less boat land him in deep water. Of course he cannot swim. Nor can he see Frodo who is trying to save him. The danger in which Sam places himself typifies his willingness to sacrifice himself for Frodo.

Reinforcement of Themes

Such confrontations reinforce the general **themes** which Tolkien has been promoting throughout the novel. The strength of men frequently corrupts both self and others as is seen in the case of Boromir's succumbing to the power of the ring. Free will Frodo exhibits admirably to illustrate the author's belief that individuals may indeed choose the way in which they will go. Power often sways people's decisions as Boromir's fancies about victories in Minas Tirith tell the reader. Frodo has a visionary role as he views the signs of war all over from the throne of the mountain kings, resembling "a lost child." Orcs are coming out of their holes. Elves and Men and beasts are fighting. Smoke arises near Lorien. All kinds of warriors battle as the Dark Lord gains power. From a point of great fear about his mission Frodo goes on to develop the necessary courage to make a decision about what to do about the ring with the assistance of the sight of evil. He chooses to do his duty as ringbearer. The **theme** of the love of man for man emerges clearly here in Sam's stubborn insistence on accompanying Frodo on his journey.

Characterization

Sam's devotion is ever deepening. He is even beginning to feel some instinct toward a sense of destiny - that he must go with Frodo. A strong compulsion to do this almost costs him his life and the reader begins to see clearly that Sam will indeed lay down his life for his friend.

Boromir, now the antithesis of good, bears the disfigurement of evil on his raging face and his gleaming eyes as selfish greed and corruption cause him to attack Frodo.

Frodo becomes a Christ-like figure. As he emerges victor over the awful power of the ring, the little hobbit is kneeling. He is not sure what he cried out when the Eye came upon him, but it might be, "Verily, I come. I come to you," echoing biblical language. A purity of purpose and selflessness surface in the little hobbit who determines to go on his mission alone.

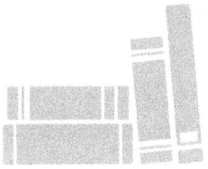

THE FELLOWSHIP OF THE RING

CHARACTERIZATION AND CRITICS

CHARACTERIZATION IN "THE FELLOWSHIP OF THE RING"

An analysis of the characterization in this novel will reveal a leading figure, Frodo Baggins, surrounded by two circles of supporting casts, his immediate companions in the Fellowship and the units of figures whom they encounter on their mission. Each of the characters functions in the work for at least one definite purpose.

THE FELLOWSHIP

Aragorn

Appearing first as Strider, Aragorn has spent seventy years scouring the countryside for the enemy, Sauron, and has collected much knowledge of the geography and various people. This enables him to serve as scout for the company and, more importantly, to impart his wisdom to the advantage of the fellowship. As a kingly figure who will someday be restored to his throne according to the prophecy, he embodies the virtues of courage, goodness, strength, and wisdom as befitting a ruler of medieval literature. His one-time capture of Gollum evidences his skill in curbing the enemy. His chaste love affair with Arwen, Elrond's daughter, reflects his noble sacrifice to the causes of duty.

Boromir

Boromir, strictly a warrior who thrives on life by the sword, appears at the Council of Elrond to find the answer to his brother's dream about a broken sword and halfling. In this role he furnishes the reader the answer to the puzzle piece in which Aragorn is to become king again and Frodo will be the ringbearer. Boromir's succumbing to the power of the ring strengthens the author's case for the evil power of the ring which produces an irresistible urge to dominate. Boromir the possessed becomes repentant.

Gandalf

Appearing first as a comical wizard with a bag of magic tricks, Gandalf soon emerges as a protector of the ringbearer and a source of invaluable wisdom from his store of ancient lore. Gandalf, a moving force setting in action the mission to destroy the ring, resembles the Biblical Moses as a leader. His staff, possessed of magic qualities, lights the way of the frightened band in the dark halls of Dwarrowdelf, or Durin's Khazad-dum. He sacrificially saves the Fellowship from the hideous monster, the Balrog, plunging into an unknown abyss resembling Christ's descent into hell, leaving the mourning Fellowship to the leadership of Aragorn.

Gimli

Gimli, who makes his first appearance at the Council of Elrond, represents a people, the Dwarves, different from men and hobbits and disliked by Elves. He signifies the transforming power of love as his friendship with the Elf Legolas deepens into a beautiful and lasting devotion. Gimli's adoration of Galadriel the Lady of Lorien results from the love and understanding which she shows the dwarf, a traditional enemy. This attachment, representing the Christian concept of brotherhood among all people, also follows the medieval practice of courtly love which features the worship of a flawless lady, usually married to someone else.

Merry (Meriodac Brandybuck)

Merry, a long-time friend of Frodo, joins the Fellowship on its mission, typifying the youthful adventurer whose mind is incapable of understanding the high purpose of the task. Merry often provides comic relief and embodies the tremendously human qualities which hobbits have. The reader easily identifies with Merry in his love of creature comforts and fun and in his fears of the unknown. Merry's insight into Frodo's dedication to destroying the ring makes him the agent to unfold the ringbearer's plan. Merry takes over mundane duties such as serving supper and gathering ponies for the perilous journey. His role, initially quite prominent, diminishes as figures of greater stature come in to the novel.

Pippin (Peregrine Took)

The character of Pippin complements Merry in many ways. Both have long been friends of Frodo. Both hobbits possess a natural exuberance. Pippin exhibits more childlike tendencies. For example, he falls asleep early in the evening with the Elves and is quietly carried off to his bed (bower) like a small infant. His impulsiveness in mistaking the calcified trolls for real trolls implicitly warns against innocence which leads to danger. Pippin assists the author in conveying his **theme** about the dangers of innocence.

Sam (Samwise Gamgee)

Sam, the hobbit, assumes a role of tremendous importance, being close companion and faithful servant of Frodo. His occupation in the Shire as gardener indicates Tolkien's belief in good emanating from close contract with the soil. Sam's character does more developing than most of the figures in the Fellowship. His sheer fear of travel into the unknown at first reveals him as very human. His devotion to Frodo grows. He weeps at his master's orc wound. He springs to Frodo's defense, either figuratively or literally. He begins in the eyes of the reader to lose himself in his service to the ringbearer and his mission. He finally actually risks his life by nearly drowning in his efforts to follow Frodo to the Mount of Doom rather than to let him go alone. The Path Sam chooses shows nobility and devotion which develop, as the story evolves, as heart-warming Christian virtues.

CHARACTERS IN COMMUNITIES

Farmer Maggot

Although the mushroom farmer appears in only one chapter, he functions as a creature close to the soil who brings good to the hobbits. He ties Frodo the ringbearer in strikingly with Bilbo, the ringfinder, by calling the hobbit traveler a thief because, as a child, he has stolen mushrooms from Farmer Maggot. Bilbo was known as "the burglar" on his expedition with the dwarves. When he warns of the danger of the Black Riders on Frodo's trail, his omens take on chilling reality because the farmer is a down-to-earth hobbit, allied with no supernatural forces. To stress this point, Tolkien has Tom Bombadil call Farmer Maggot "Muddy-feet."

The atmosphere at the supper table exudes rural warmth. Mrs. Maggot bustles in a housewifely fashion and the group, including several sons and daughters, enjoy a sumptuous meal featuring mushrooms which hobbits adore. This scene represents the last real touch with ordinary life for the hobbits and the Maggot family, the last ordinary creatures whom the sojourners will encounter in their adventures.

Tom Bombadil

Tom Bombadil stands out as an anomaly in Tolkien's secondary world, a kind of natural spirit so unfettered that the ring has no power over him. There is an agelessness about this quaint creature who looks like a man and wears colorful blue clothing, a pointed hat and yellow boots. Merriment and good heartedness abound within his jolly heart. He serves as a veritable steward, being the master of the Old Forest with much control over natural and supernatural creatures without a strong sense of ownership. He acts as a steward for the hobbits, a steward with the uncanny ability to feel their needs when in danger and bail them out of trouble with his strange, benevolent powers. As a protector he proves to be undeniably strong. He is, in fact, an agent of fate.

Tom's wife, Goldberry, likewise belongs to the world of natural sprites, being the daughter of the River-woman of the Withywindle. Lovely, yellow-haired, Goldberry possesses an assuring serenity like that of a madonna. Her maternal role reveals her comforting the hobbits with words of peace which echo the New Testament. Tom and Goldberry offer their sylvan home in the golden glow of candles as a haven for the hobbits, one step removed from Farmer Maggot's household. A clear drink in their bowls makes them give away to immediate song. The reader begins to progress to an acceptance of Second World dwellings removed from the customary types encountered so far.

Barliman Butterbur

The innkeeper at the Sign of the Prancing Pony offers a transition-type abode, ordinary on the surface with sinister omens underneath. The balding, red-faced Barliman flusters and blusters about providing for the hobbits' physical needs. His role as a Man of Bree ties him to the world of the ordinary but he also serves as a link with the supernatural because of his connection with Gandalf. His forgetfulness about Gandalf's letter to Frodo would lead the reader to believe that Barliman had no real thought of anything but the mundane business of hostelry life. He represents a liaison unawares. This speculation gains strength when the reader remembers that it is Frodo himself who introduces the supernatural element into the conviviality of the evening in the public room at the inn by putting on the ring and disappearing.

Elrond

Elrond of the Elves presides over what is known as the Last Homely House east of the Sea and exercises great healing powers over Frodo's orc wound. The Last Homely House, perfect in every detail, offers food, sleep, storytelling, and singing to banish all weariness and fear. As Lord of Rivendell, the great Elven kingdom, Elrond heads up the Council which decides the future of the ring. He represents the medieval bard, filled with ancient lore about the ring, which he imparts at the meeting at great length. His agelessness has enabled him to live through many wars and to recall the history of the One Ring for the assembly. Elrond is a Solomon-type figure for his might lies in his wisdom. Out of the infinite wisdom he does not appoint Frodo to carry the ring to Mordor. Frodo offers of his own free will although he does not know the way. Elrond accepts the offer.

Arwen

Arwen represents ideal womanhood although she is of the Elven folk, being the daughter of Elrond. When Aragorn meets her at Rivendell, she is so lovely that she is said to resemble Luthien and is called Undomiel or Evening Star. One look from her light-filled eyes makes Aragorn fall instantly in love with her. She sings in her clear voice a lovely Elven song about Elbereth. Arwen embodies the virtues of Una in Spenser's Faerie Queen. Her aloof perfection makes it difficult for the reader to identify with her. Tolkien's handling of women characters totters weakly somewhere between a stiff idealism and a plain inadequacy.

Glorfindel

Second in greatness only to Elrond among the Elves, Glorfindel takes over the role of protector of the hobbits as he fights the Nine Riders who compose the dread Nazgul at the Ford of Bruinen on the way to Rivendell. His horse, Asfolath, bears Frodo to safety at his master's command. Glorfindel appears to the hobbits as a radiant rider, clad in white raiment, an otherworldly figure to bring them aid. He serves as a liaison character to prepare the reader for the Elf-land of Rivendell.

Celeborn

Lord of the Elves called the Galadrim, who live in tree houses, Celeborn rules in Lorien, an idyllic spot where the hobbits have a respite from the dangers of their mission. Celeborn comes off as a weak Elrond minus the great store of wisdom belonging to his colleague over in Rivendell.

Galadriel

Celeborn's Lady of Lorien, Galadriel considerably up-stages her ruler-husband. As a Tolkien lady-character she uniquely becomes alive. She allows Frodo and Sam to look into the magic mirror, a helpful source of information. She lavishes gifts upon the Company at the time of their departure. Frodo's present, a phial containing the light of Earendil's star set in waters from Galadriel's own fountain, has special significance as a life-giving agent. Beauty and gentleness distinguish Galadriel who at first unsettles Frodo with a nameless fear of her. She has the power to refuse the ring. As Frodo knows her better, the eerie quality which causes him apprehension earlier, disappears. Love and trust seal the relationship.

CHARACTERS OF EVIL

Sauron

The Dark Lord, the Lord of Mordor, who is casting the shadow of evil over Middle Earth, covets the One Ring in the possession of Frodo. Sauron, obsessed with the urgent desire to dominate, for a time has passed as the Necromancer of Dol Guldur, which Saruman protects. Sauron's names vary. Gollum refers to him as the Black Hand. The Eye, the Great Eye and Red Eye rank among his sobriquets which indicate his watchfulness for the opportunity to grasp a victim and/or to overcome the earth. Sauron, the Lord of the Rings, interestingly enough, never actually appears in *The Fellowship of the Ring*, evidencing Tolkien's belief that the reader can construct a much more monstrous image of evil out of his own mind rather than out of a compedium of the author's adjectives. Since Sauron reduces the abstraction of evil to personification, he provides Tolkien with a viable adversary. (His name comes from the Greek base for lizard, suggesting the biblical serpent.)

Saruman

The erstwhile white wizard, who once stood as the greatest of the order of Istari, represents the perversion of goodness, conveying Tolkien's theory that all evil has its roots in goodness. Saruman's attempt to corrupt Gandalf leads to his dismissal from the order of wizards. His double dealings deter the actions of the White Council for a time until his duplicity can be discovered.

He calls himself Saruman, the Many Colored, wearing a robe of bright hues which symbolically represents his perversion from the white of purity to the stained colors of sins.

Orcs

Evil creatures of a strange breed stalk the Fellowship on its journey, carrying out the orders of their master, Sauron. A mocking counterpart of the Elves, orcs show fierce skills as warriors of great endurance, dark, hideous, fanged assailants with squat legs and squinty eyes. Hating beauty and light, they thrive in darkness as is typical of evil with Tolkien's symbolism.

Black Riders

The chief servants of Sauron, the Black Riders, also known as the Nazgul, are searching for Frodo and the ring. In one encounter Frodo receives a wound from the Lord of the Nazgul. At another meeting the horses of the evil agents drown in the floodwaters of the Bruinen. Like orcs, the Black Riders thrive in darkness. They use the Black Breath, the dread stench emanating from them which reduces their victim to a coma. Invisible sources of terror, said to be blind, they communicate in either dreadful cries in the night or in their own harsh tongue, the Black Speech. The Black Riders, elusive and fearful, speak for Tolkien as evil agents who have the upper hand over good in the world.

The Balrog

A terrible monster, not unlike a griffin with vast wingspread and a deadly whip, rules in Khazad-Dum until Gandalf, in hand-to-hand conflict, destroys him. The Balrog serves Tolkien as Gandalf's evil guide into the hell in which he seemingly perishes in *The Fellowship of the Ring*.

LEADING CHARACTER

Frodo

In presenting his leading character, Frodo, The hobbit ringbearer, Tolkien places him initially in the simple, rural environment of the Shire as verdant as the Garden of Eden. Frodo appears then as Adam before the fall. The decline of the world from greatness shortly becomes axiomatic. The ringbearer obviously contrasts with the figure of the mythic hero; he is indeed the inversion of the mythic hero, totally unsuited to life by the sword and the shield. He says, "'I am not made for perilous quests.'"

The crucial chapter, "The Shadow of the Past," brings the first inklings of change in Frodo's character as his desire to join Bilbo grows. A strange restlessness bids him seek lands outside the Shire. Simultaneously Gandalf bathes the surprised little hobbit in knowledge about the ring which Bilbo never knew. Frodo learns that he will deal with the shadow of evil encompassing Middle Earth in a historical cycle which will repeat events of the past. Tolkien is possibly telling his reader that in the endless battle against evil in the world, a new kind of hero is deemed necessary. The hobbit, an unexpected figure to make a quest to redeem his fellowmen, appears naive, somewhat curious and certainly powerless. (For that matter, hobbits as a rule have little interest in power as men do.)

Actually the Fellowship brings out dual quests - Frodo's mission to toss the ring in the Cracks of Doom at Orodruin, the

Fire-mountain, and Aragorn's task of returning as ruler to his kingdom. Frodo's quest takes precedence over the other in *The Fellowship of the Ring* though both are intertwined.

Frodo's early sense of wanderlust prompts an inner compulsion which Tolkien uses to express his belief in the elect - Frodo has been chosen as the ringbearer within an overall scheme which promotes order in the universe. Also an act of free will on Frodo's part forces him to accept the rule though at times he decries his fate. "'I would that it had not happened in my time.'"

Tolkien shows his respect for man's inner resources when Frodo from time to time finds within himself unsuspected courage and capabilities to war against evil. Frodo even questions his own physical stamina and the strength of his will but at the times of decision-making, a reassuring and growing determination to destroy the ring proves that he is developing as a character. After his orc wound Frodo's sense become sharper and warns him of things which cannot be seen. As the novel progresses, the hobbit hero appears more and more independent of the other members of the company and is often physically alone.

One distinguishing aspect in the makeup of Frodo concerns his dreams. In the instance of his vision about Gandalf he sees the wizard's escape from Orthanc. An uneasy dream presages his imminent attack by the Black Riders. Another dream about two pinpoints of light coming toward him eerily heralds the vigilance of Gollum.

Frodo's inspiring sense of wonder caps this little earthly character with an exciting quality. In Lothlorien, "a timeless land that did not fade or change or fall into forgetfulness," Frodo delights in feeling wood, in the living tree itself. He finds

Aragorn's response to the region quite similar to his own. The unearthly loveliness of Arwen, the Evenstar of her people, overwhelms him. His experiencing wonder shows his empathy for a better, purer and unstained world.

Frodo remains sexless throughout the novel. As master of Bag End, he stays a bachelor enjoying male companionship. The all-masculine Fellowship operates on the concept of brotherly love and service. Frodo, the key figure in the band of travelers, provides his companions with a sense of unified purpose and a sense of meaning in the world to which everyone relates.

In the novel's adventuresome pattern of pursuit and escape, Frodo finally achieves an epiphany, that is, a moment of supreme perception of the natural world's approaching a divine one. After his threatening encounter with Boromir, Frodo experiences an **epic** and panoramic vision. Seated in the chair of the Guardian Kings of Gondor at the top of Amon Hen in the Seat of Seeing, he beholds the embattled world covered with orcs, Lorien in smoke and the Beornings' land in flames. The Fortress of Sauron rises impenetrable and powerful. Hopeless, Frodo then feels the Eye. Momentary tensions between evil power and his own will contest within him. As agent free to choose, the ringbearer escapes the Eye and vows, "'I will do now what I must.'" Furthermore, his instinct to save his friends and to sacrifice himself flowers into full determination. Invisible to escape and band, he goes by unseen like Bilbo's leaving the Shire, "less than a rustle in the wind."

Critics Respond To "The Fellowship" Of The Ring

A remarkable unanimity of praise exists in the reviews of *The Lord of the Rings* though occasionally derogatory notices have appeared. The bulk of Tolkien criticism certainly leads one to conclude that the author is a charmer as a narrator and occupies a unique spot in a modern-day literary annals. Widespread adulation of the British author did not sweep the United States immediately upon the publication of the trilogy by Houghton Mifflin without an American copyright. Despite the persistent refusal of Houghton Mifflin to allow reprints in paperback, Ace Books ordered a printing of 50,000 copies of The *Lord of the Rings* to hit the marketplace in April, 1955. Sales spiraled so high that Ace ordered another 100,000 copies of *The Fellowship of the Ring* as well as 150,000 copies of *The Two Towers* and *The Return of the King*. Great controversy, spearheaded by an irate Tolkien, evolved over payments. This promptly dissolved with the reprinter's offer to pay Tolkien full royalties. Ballantine Books then released authorized versions, 97,000 copies of each novel composing the trilogy as well as 200,000 copies of *The Hobbit*.

The publishing controversy significantly fanned the fires of interest in the trilogy, making the works available to many for a more reasonable price than the hardback books. Subsequently the Tolkien Society of America appeared under the leadership of Harvard student Dick Plotz, attracting countless college-age fans. Subsequently numerous other societies have covered the United States and attest the popularity of J. R. R. Tolkien in America.

Mathewson: Student Appeal

Joseph Mathewson in "The Hobbit Habit" in *Esquire* (September, 1966) argues ably the reasons why students of the Sixties prefer Tolkien to J. D. Salinger and William Golding. *The Catcher in the Rye* caught the fancy of avid readers for a time with its premise that all adults are phony. Students of the Sixties, who find adults working assiduously for the same goals as the young, must reject Salinger. Their idealism about remaking the world into a better place causes them to condemn Golding's thesis that people, given a second chance to start all over again, would surely fail all over again.

As for the world of students of the Sixties, Mathewson writes, "They may well want to escape from it occasionally. The best escape is not just a way though, but a means of assurance, too: It's better to go down a ladder than to jump from a sixth floor window. And the great appeal of the Tolkien books may be that they offer both, not only page after page of faraway Middle Earth but also victory of good over evil in a struggle where the lines are as clearly drawn as they were in Selma, Alabama. Having found such a febrifuge, the students have naturally done what they could to make it a lasting one, absorbing its every detail and coming in effect to believe in Middle Earth as an alternate reality."

Schroth: Compelling Craftsmanship

Although Raymond A. Schroth criticizes the trilogy as "too long, too cluttered, too much" in *America* (February 18, 1967), he admires the author as a craftsman. "... Tolkien's poetic and narrative gifts are so compelling that many readers move anxiously through the magnificently described events half-convinced they are having an esoteric, as well, as pleasurable, experience."

He acknowledges criticisms of the work and immediately refutes them with perceptive observations. "Still, to me, the value of Tolkien is not the very dubious value of psychological escape; but a reinvitation to myth: a symbolic representation in story form of a present reality, drawing our attention to a hitherto unnoticed dimension of our common existence. Myth reveals truth, just as a smile or a gesture reveals love.

"To some critics, Middle Earth is anti-feminine, anti-technological and anti-human ... there is a conservative retreat to a simplistic view of reality where the lines between good and evil are clearly drawn and the irresponsible reader is freed from personal involvement or choice. To others, the excursion is more like a spiritual retreat. In the hobbit Shire and in the journey down the Great River, we recoup our psychological resources by rediscovering, for once, a world over which we have at least some imaginative control. Then we bounce back, like Frodo, and muddle through life with our ordinary talents to cataclysmic victory."

Wilson: "Oo, Those Awful Orcs"

"There is never much development in the episodes; you simply go on getting more of the same thing. Dr. Tolkien has little skill at narrative and no instinct for literary form. The characters talk a story-book language that might have come out of Howard Pyle, and as personalities they do not impose themselves.... There are Black Riders, of whom everyone is terrified, but who never seem anything but specters. There are dreary, hovering birds-think of it, horrible birds of prey! There are ogreish disgusting Orcs who, however, rarely get to the point of committing any overt acts ... What one misses in all these terrors is any trace of concrete reality. The preternatural, to be effective, should be given some sort of solidity, a real presence, recognizable features-like Gulliver, like Gogol, like Poe ..." Thus writes Edmund Wilson in *The Nation* (April 14, 1956).

Straight: Haunting, Ennobling

Michael Straight writes of "The Fantastic World of Professor Tolkien" in *New Republic* (January 16, 1956): "It was a haunting and ennobling world, held together by inner tension, and so the spell lasted while the fate of his world remained in doubt ... His [Tolkien's] preparation is immersion in Welsh, Norse, Gaelic, Scandinavian and Germanic folklore ... the universality and timelessness of its plot give to it allegorical significance ... It is the struggle between good and evil that Tolkien sets apart, through fantasy, from superficial detail. Evil, in the form of Sauron, is man's rebellion against Providence, his attempt to become the Lord of a world he did not make...

"He [Tolkien] possesses elvish craft. He adds to it the scholar's perspective and the humanist's faith. And yet he never allows his magical balance of mystery and perception to be lost. For these reasons his world of fantasy is more gripping than the events that occur next door, say at Ten North Frederick. For Tolkien's fantasy does not obscure, but illuminates the inner consistency of reality. There are very few works of genius in recent literature. This is one."

Elliott: Astonishing

"His prose is fibrous with high seriousness and he has a positively incantatory way with proper names," states Charles Elliott in "Can America Kick the Hobbit? The Tolkien Caper" in *Life* (February 24, 1967). "His real forte, however, is the construction of historical and philological sand castles of astonishing complexity. He surrounds his tale with enough pseudo-scholarly paraphernalia to float a new edition of Macpherson's Ossian."

Halle: Inventive Genius

Louis J. Halle in "History Through the Mind's Eye" in the *Saturday Review of Literature* (January 28, 1956) asserts that "Dr. Tolkien's inventiveness if of that order which, because it challenges the credulity of us ordinary mortals, we call genius ... The two prime facts of Middle Earth, if the reviewer may offer his own interpretation, are power and its consequence, suffering ... In the historian's view power is not a neutral element that can be used for good or evil. It is always evil, for it enables the wicked to dominate the world, or, in the hands of the good is inescapably corrupting."

Colby: Tolkien and Dragons

Writing on "J. R. R. Tolkien" in the *Wilson Library Bulletin* (June, 1957), Vineta Colby describes *The Fellowship of the Ring* as "Frodo's first attempts to destroy the ring after learning of its sinister power." Had this reviewer described the novel as the beginning of Frodo's attempt to destroy the ring, she might have come closer to the mark. Of Tolkien's love affair with dragons she quotes that he revealed that as a child, "'I desired dragons with a profound desire. Of course I in my timid body did not wish to have them in the neighborhood, intruding into my relatively safe world, in which it was, for instance, possible to read stories in peace of mind, free from fear. But the world that contained even the imagination of Fafnir was richer and more beautiful, at whatever cost of peril.'"

Davenport: "Best Book of the Century"

Calling the book a "Christian parable," Guy Davenport in his article in *National Review* (September 23, 1973), states that of the trilogy "we can easily say that it is the best book of the century, though the greatest is *Ulysses*, and Lewis' *The Human Age* is the book we deserve most to be remembered for … Tolkien dared to resuscitate the romance, a form requiring the genius of a Rabelais or Spenser, a form which was shattered after its brilliant flowering in the hands of Boiardo and Ariosto by the publication of *Don Quixote*."

Davenport introduces an interesting personal note. "Allen Barnett of Shelbyville, Kentucky, classmate of Tolkien's at college, may have been his only friend to survive World War I. Tolkien loved to hear about Kentuckians, their contempt for shoes, their fields of tobacco, their countrified ancient English names like Proudfoot and Baggins … If the Shire is flavored with touches of Kentucky, we need but know that Tolkien was born in South Africa to see what he was remembering in the lacy golden trees of Lothlorien. Not since Spenser has an English writer had so gorgeous an imagination."

Time: Cultural and Social Influence

Time (September 17, 1973) notes that "Scholars and critics had at first admired [Tolkien's] books while tracing down literary influences that ranged from Buchan … to *Beowulf*. Then, with such popularity, [the first paperback edition of the three volumes of the Ring sold close to 500,000 copies,] the story was denounced as escapist fantasy, its success owlishly attributed to 'irrational adulation' and 'nonliterary cultural and social phenomena.'"

Sklar. "Art and History"

"Tolkien's trilogy resembles the Anglo-Saxon chronicles he studied as a scholar. *The Lord of the Rings* is a work of art but it is also history-and it bears comparison to the works of Gibbon or Parkman more readily than it does to other novels. The great historians are equally artists and builders of worlds. Gibbon's Rome and Parkman's French America are worlds as strange and distant from our own as Tolkien's Middle Earth. On the level of great historical narratives it matters little whether the events described can be absolutely verified; what matters far more is the historian's attitude toward his world and his treatment of it." So writes Robert Sklar in *The Nation* (May 8, 1967).

He continues to develop the concept of the trilogy as history. "As a work of history *The Lord of the Rings* is distinctly Spenglerian in tone. Tolkien has created a historical world with a comprehensive erudition and a philosophical audacity few historians since Spengler have been able to match-and with a sense of tragic destiny nearly equal to Spengler's."

Norman: Tolkien on the Hobbit

Tolkien responded to Philip Norman writing for *The New York Times Magazine* (January 15, 1967) about his intention of having children as his audience. "Children aren't a class. They are merely human beings at different stages of maturity. All of them have a human intelligence which even at its lowest is a pretty wonderful thing, and the entire world in front of them."

Norman states that: "He modeled his hobbits on the Sarehole people, which means that they must have been gentle amblers, not really fond of adventures but very fond of their food. Tolkien himself likes plain meals and beer; "none of that cuisine mystique. Beer, cheese, butter and pastry; the occasional glass of burgundy."

Tolkien remarked, "'Hobbits ... have what you might call universal morals. I have said they are examples of natural philosophy and natural religion.'" Norman adds, "They are certainly capable of extraordinary bravery and humaneness: living in burrows, their creator declares, does not amount to anything like an animal kink."

Tolkien also notes, "'The imagined beings have their insides on the outside; they are visible souls. And Man as a whole, Man pitted against the Universe, have we seen him at all till we see that he is like a hero in a fairy tale?'"

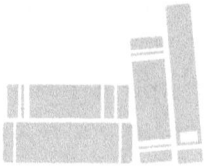

THE FELLOWSHIP OF THE RING

ESSAY QUESTIONS AND ANSWERS

Question: Discuss elements of fantasy or myth which appear in *The Fellowship Of The Ring*.

Answer: *The Fellowship of the Ring* contains elements of both myth and fantasy. Aragorn, Strider, the Ranger heir of Isildur, embodies the characteristics of a mythical king of medieval literature such as King Arthur. As the wisest man of his time with great experience in traveling far and wide, he assumes the leadership of the Fellowship after Gandalf's disappearance at Khazad-Dum. His healing powers do much to help Frodo's orc wound. Aragorn owns a magic sword, Anduril, which was once broken and is now reforged.

Aragorn is on a mission to find his kingdom and be restored to the throne. More important than that, his true dedication to wiping out evil in the world puts him on a level with the mythical kings of ancient times as do his courage, prowess, and stamina in the midst of hardships.

The hobbits as creatures of the author's imagination provide ample evidence of Tolkien's use of fantasy. Springing from a well-farmed community, these small (two to four feet high) individuals tend to be quite plump since they eat about six meals a day and live in a leisurely fashion. Smoking pipe weed supplies them with pleasure. They enjoy parties and gift giving. Bright-eyed and redcheeked, they wear bright colored clothing. Their most distinguishing feature is their tough feet, covered with thick curling hair

While hobbits have a charm of their own, orcs, another fantastic creation of the author, possess qualities only to repel. Black, evil creatures, they are short, bow-legged, squat. Their swarthy faces grimace. They hate daylight and operate only in the darkness. Their speech sounds guttural and harsh. They thrive on open warfare against good, being servants of the Dark Lord, Sauron.

Tolkien treats Elves, fantastic creatures not altogether original with the author, as the noblest breed of people in Middle Earth. Different from Shakespeare, Tolkien makes his Elves tall (six feet), graceful beings of great strength. They seem ageless.

These Elves dwell in idyllic spots and love trees, music and all gentle, harmonious things. They worship the stars and starlight seems to emanate from their lovely forms.

Question: Discuss the significant **themes** of *The Fellowship of the Ring*.

Answer: The major **theme** which Tolkien uses is the problem of evil. The great power of evil is threatening to overcome the world. Most of the time evil is stronger than good although good does exist as a vital element in Tolkien's mind. Good, by contrast to the dark pervasive qualities of Tolkien's concept of evil, seems shaky, small and weak, tried in an almost unwinnable contest. It is possible that man may win for a time but the vigilance and battle against evil never cease.

On the plus side in the conflict the **theme** of man's sense of responsibility and his free will emerge as an affirmation of good. Man (or hobbit like Frodo) feels inwardly compelled to do his duty in the interest of the common welfare. Man is free to choose how he will act. Tolkien ties into this his concept of an overall purpose operating in the universe. He believes often that man is chosen to act in a certain way. Chance and chaos do not figure in his thinking. Love forms another affirmative aspect, especially the devotion of man for his fellowman. This impinges on the Christian concept of laying down one's life for a friend.

Tolkien preaches anti-materialism in a low key. High virtues are matters of beauty and spirit rates much higher on his scale of values than gold and jewels which always seem to spell havoc to him. Tolkien equates goodness with the soil. He appears reactionary, preferring simple, rural-agrarian type societies to industrialized cities where technological progress reigns and rules out individuality. He figures that present-day scientific and technological advances are reducing the world to a wasteland of destruction and sterility. Tolkien protests strongly against the modern age as insuring the ruin of the individual.

Question: Is Tolkien's use of symbolism effective? Support your position with examples from the text.

Answer: Tolkien's use of symbolism is effective because of its traditional simplicity. Different from many modern authors who construct their own symbolic systems outside of any literary heritage, Tolkien follows the age-old prescriptions. For example, black represents evil. Evil moves in the shadows of night, despising light. Orcs, Black Riders, and Sauron, who is called the Dark Lord, exemplify this.

On the other hand, white for purity and green for goodness and life go with the virtuous, high-minded characters. Goldberry exists in a bower of green, sometimes clad in green, sometimes in white. The Elven royalty usually appears in white raiment with a star-light sheen. The White Tree of Gondor, which has withered and died in Minas Anor, signifies the imminent death of civilization if the Dark Lord cannot be checked. Trees to Tolkien represent life.

The hobbits Tolkien uses to represent the average little man who must struggle against evil, at times ineptly but always surprisingly courageously. Hobbits experience desires for pleasure and duty-shirking just as the average person does but an inner compunction drives them on to act for the greater good of all. The hobbit is literally small, as man is not in actual appearance, but the hobbit is the visual representation of man as he really is-quite small in a cosmic struggle. Hobbits exhibit such exquisitely human qualities that we realize that, no matter how weak and tempted the little man may be, Tolkien finds his fellow creatures lovable after all.

Question: What are Tolkien's main methods of characterization? Give examples of at least three characters from the text.

Answer: Tolkien characterizes his cast of players by description of their personal appearance, by dialogue, by giving their innermost thoughts, and by showing them in action. Frodo, being the leading character, becomes quite alive for us immediately as soon as Bilbo leaves the Shire. He shows sadness at his uncle's departure and assumes his responsibility as master of Bag End as a preface to his responsibility as ringbearer. Frodo's conversations with Gandalf indicate immediately certain trepidations which will dog his steps all the way on his mission.

Frodo is a developing character growing from a little hobbit who has just passed his tweens to a mature man challenged with the ordeal of destroying the One Ring. His sense of responsibility deepens the substance of his makeup. He says to Elrond, "'I will take the ring ... though I do not know the way.'" Frodo, infinitely small, helpless, forces himself to do his duty. When he needs courage, he somehow finds it inside.

While nobility of purpose strengthens Frodo, the effects of evil also leave their scars. The orc wound visibly indicates the life-sapping power of evil. There are times, too, when Frodo experiences the strange power of the ring but we see him growing in strength and determination to exert his own will against it. He also grows in dedication to his colleagues, not wanting to endanger their lives, willing to sacrifice his own on a lonely mission.

Tolkien devotes little space to Frodo's personal appearance because of the detailed description of the hobbit in the Prologue.

Gandalf is also a developing character. When first seen, he rides into the Shire with a wagon load of tricky firecrackers for Bilbo's party. He appears at the time to be a run-of-the-mill wizard with a pointed hat, white beard and bushy eyebrows, employing the usual bag of tricks. However, it turns out that Gandalf has spent long years battling the evil Sauron. In the meeting at Elrond's Hall of Fire Gandalf tells the whole story of the One Ring.

His dialogue, composed of both long narrations and short conversations, always conveys great wisdom.

He serves as a protector for the Fellowship, being a wise guide to lead them with his staff through the ordeals promised on the Quest of Mount Doom. Gandalf the Grey shows himself externally for the most part through Frodo's eyes. We cannot be sure what the enigmatic wizard is thinking.

His leadership role takes him into personal conflict with the Balrog monster and demonstrates his majestic and impressive selflessness in trying to protect the Fellowship. However, the monster causes Gandalf to fall into the abyss and he is mourned by the travelers as their lost and beloved leader.

Aragorn is another character whom the reader sees externally. He is, in fact, somewhat stereotyped as the warrior-hero out of ancient literature. First introduced as Strider, Aragorn shows signs of wear and travel. He has spent many years in the wilderness tracking down Sauron and has built up a wealth of knowledge about the region and its people. He intuitively knows that Frodo has the ring and instantly begins to serve as a helper and protector.

As he moves away from his role as Strider, his handsome clothing make him a much more impressive figure. His manner of speech sounds quaint, even stilted at times. His physical stature impresses people.

When Gandalf vanishes, Aragorn takes over the leadership of the Fellowship. He exhibits remarkable healing powers with Frodo's orc wound as becomes a would-be king. His courage in the face of danger, his physical prowess, his manly bearing and even his love for the beautiful Arwen all fit him into the picture of a traditional medieval king.

Question: What special features distinguish Tolkien's literary style?

Answer: Tolkien's literary style shows a variety of features which seem extremely well suited to his subject matter. As an author he has an enormous amount of material to convey to his reader, essentially background material. He gives characters like Gandalf long speeches in which to explain past events. In the meeting at the House of Elrond Boromir, the dwarf Gloin, Aragorn and Gandalf all take turns in long monologues supplying explanations, especially about the ring.

We notice that the dialogue in *The Fellowship of the Ring* contains variety. Characters like Elrond and Galadriel of high rank speak in a dignified and archaic fashion. The little hobbits sound like ordinary Englishmen conversing informally in pubs. Their **diction** pegs them socially as people of the soil.

Tolkien makes use of much poetry for the purpose of heightening the mood of a special scene or of expressing emotions. The interjection of poems in a prose narrative is quite unusual in contemporary fiction. These poems make for easy reading with simple **rhyme** schemes, definite rhythms and, in many cases, a clear narrative thread to give the reader the story of a character, often legendary.

Tolkien uses descriptive passages very effectively. His choice of somber adjectives gives us vivid pictures of the Hall of Flame or the frightening Khazad-Dum, Durin's palace. His delightful, colorful range of adjectives brings to life lovely landscapes in the safe havens like Tom Bombadil's house or the heavenly looking Elven folk. His unusually successful **imagery** in describing landscape-either friendly or hostile-often tends to treat objects in nature as people. The scenes of conflict bristle with action verbs.

Descriptions of great numbers of varied settings add interest. We move from the verdant Shire to Farmer Maggot's mushroom farm and on to several different regions peopled by supernatural creatures. In contrast to this come terrifying scenes in the Old Forest, on journeys in the dark, in a fierce blizzard, in the flood tide of the Bruinen. Tolkien uses great balance in arranging his material since he moves his band of travelers from safety to danger and back again in neat proportion.

Also, the One Ring forms the unifying force around which all sorts and kinds of actions and settings are bound together.

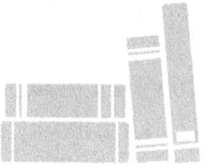

THE FELLOWSHIP OF THE RING

TOPICS FOR RESEARCH AND CRITICISM

1. The Uses of Time in *The Fellowship of the Ring*.

2. Tolkien's Concept of the Meaning of Innocence and Experience.

3. Tolkien's Approach to the Characterization of Women.

4. *The Fellowship of the Ring* as **Epic** and Myth.

5. The Hobbits' Way of Life: The Case for and against the Shire.

6. The Symbolism of Evil in *The Fellowship of the Ring*.

7. Tolkien's Use of Personification as a Literary Technique.

8. Symbolism of Good in *The Fellowship of the Ring*.

9. The Effectiveness of Tolkien's Use of Fantasy.

10. The Kinds of Historical **Allusions** in *The Fellowship of the Ring* and their Functions.

11. Tolkien's Notions about Communities and Community Life.

12. The influences of Medieval Literature in *The Fellowship of the Ring*.

13. *The Fellowship of the Ring* as Allegory.

14. Tolkien's Major Theme.

15. Tolkien's Portrayal of Heroes.

16. Tolkien's Uses of Poetry and Song.

17. The Types of Love Found in *The Fellowship of the Ring*.

18. The Comparison and the Contrast of Middle Earth to the Modern World.

19. Tolkien's Concept of Power and its Uses.

20. Tolkien's View of an Overall Purpose in the Universe.

21. The Significance of Seeing Middle Earth from the Hobbit's Point of View in *The Fellowship of the Ring*.

22. Tolkien's Manner of Character Development.

23. The Significance of Galadriel's Gifts to the Hobbits.

24. Death and Decay as Portrayed in *The Fellowship of the Ring*.

25. The Significance of the Title of *The Fellowship of the Ring*.

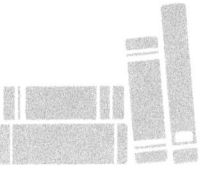

BIBLIOGRAPHY

Editions Of Tolkien's Fiction

The Hobbit, or, There and Back Again.

London: George Allen and Unwin, Ltd., 1937.

Boston: Houghton Mifflin Company, 1938.

New York: Ballantine Books, Inc., 1965.

The Lord of the Rings, a trilogy composed of *The Fellowship of the Ring, The Two Towers,* and *The Return of the King.*

London: George Allen and Unwin, Ltd., 1954-55.

Boston: Houghton Mifflin Company, 1955-56. Revision, 1967.

New York: Ballantine Books, Inc., 1965.

Tree and Leaf.

London: George Allen and Unwin, Ltd., 1964.

Boston: Houghton Mifflin Company, 1965.

Farmer Giles of Ham

London: George Allen and Unwin, Ltd., 1949.

The Homecoming of Beorhtnoth Beorhthelm's Son.

Essays and Studies for 1953, copyrighted by the English Association, 1953.

The Adventures of Tom Bombadil. (Poems).

London: George Allen and Unwin, Ltd., 1962.

Smith of Wooton Major (with Farmer Giles of Ham)

New York: Ballantine Books, Inc., 1969.

The Tolkien Reader.

New York: Ballantine Books, Inc., 1966.

Criticism Of Tolkien's Fiction

Carter, Lin. Tolkien: *A Look Behind The Lord of The Rings.* New York: Ballantine Books, Inc., 1969.

Colby, Vineta. "J. R. R. Tolkien." *Wilson Library Bulletin* (June, 1957), p. 768.

Davenport, Guy. Review. *National Review* (September 28, 1973), pp. 1042–3.

Elliott, Charles. "Can America Kick the Hobbit? The Tolkien Caper." *Life* (February 24, 1967), p. 10.

Evans, Robley. *Writers for the Seventies: J. R. R. Tolkien.* New York: Warner Paperback Library, 1972.

Foster, Robert. *A Guide to Middle Earth.* New York, Ballantine Books, Inc., 1971.

Fuller, Edmund. *Books with Men Behind Them.* New York: Random House, 1959.

Halle, Louis J. "History Through the Mind's Eye." *Saturday Review of Literature* (January 28, 1956), pp. 11–12.

Helms, Randel. *Tolkien's World.* Boston: Houghton Mifflin Company, 1974.

Hillegas, Mark R., ed. *Shadows of Imagination: The Fantasies of C. S. Lewis, J. R. R. Tolkien, and Charles Williams.* Carbondale and Edwardsville: Southern Illinois University Press, 1969.

Isaacs, Neil D. and Rose A. Zimbardo, eds. *Tolkien and the Critics.* Notre Dame: University of Notre Dame Press, 1969.

Kocher, Paul H. *Master of Middle Earth: The Fiction of J. R. R. Tolkien.* Boston: Houghton Mifflin Company, 1972.

Lobdell, Jared, ed. *A Tolkien Compass.* LaSalle: Open Court, 1974.

Mathewson, Joseph. "The Hobbit Habit." *Esquire* (September, 1966), pp. 130–1 plus.

Norman, Philip. "The Prevalence of Hobbits." *New York Times Magazine* (January 15, 1967), pp. 30–1.

Ready, William. *The Tolkien Relation.* Chicago: Henry Regnery Co., 1968.

Schroth, Raymond A. Review. *America* (February 18, 1967), p. 254.

Simpson, Catharine R. *J. R. R. Tolkien.* New York: Columbia University Press, 1969.

Sklar, Robert. Review. *Nation* (May 8, 1967), pp. 598-60.

Straight, Michael. "The Fantastic World of Professor Tolkien." *New Republic* (January 16, 1956), pp. 24-6.

Time. "Eucatastrophe." (September 17, 1973), p. 101.

Urang, Gunnar. *Shadows of Heaven: Religion and Fantasy in the Writings of C. S. Lewis, Charles Williams, and J. R. R. Tolkien.* Philadelphia: Pilgrim Press, 1971.

West, Richard C. *Tolkien Criticism: An Annotated Checklist (Bibliographies and Checklists No. 11)* Kent, Ohio: Kent State University, 1970.

Wilson, Edmund. "Oo, Those Awful Orcs!" *Nation* (April 14, 1956), pp. 312-13.

www.ingramcontent.com/pod-product-compliance
Lightning Source LLC
LaVergne TN
LVHW011717060526
838200LV00051B/2925